'YESTERDAY'

STUDIES IN BIBLICAL THEOLOGY

Second Series · 4

'YESTERDAY'

A Study of Hebrews in the Light of Chapter 13

FLOYD V. FILSON

ALEC R. ALLENSON, INC.
635 EAST OGDEN AVENUE
NAPERVILLE, ILL.

FIRST PUBLISHED 1967
PRINTED IN GREAT BRITAIN BY
ROBERT CUNNINGHAM AND SONS LTD
ALVA

CONTENTS

46809

PREFACE

THE discussion that follows is by no means a complete study of Hebrews. It does not pretend to deal with all questions that would be involved in a relatively thorough study, nor does it attempt to present the full range of available bibliography. Those who want to see how varied and extensive are the recent studies of Hebrews may turn to the important bibliographical and evaluative article by Erich Grässer entitled 'Der Hebräerbrief 1938–1963', published in *Theologische Rundschau* 30, 1964, pp. 138–236.

The attempt we make in the present study is to find and vindicate a new approach which will let us understand better the literary form, the key themes, and the basic unity of Hebrews. To put our purpose another way, we here try to let the author say what he wants to say; we do not intend to make him fit into the patterns either of our modern thought or of other New Testament writers. He shows agreements with Christian writers of his time, but he is no mere echo or duplicate of any contemporary author. It will be a great gain if we can hear him speak in his own way and let him put the emphasis on his own key ideas and aims. With great ability and skill he confronts us with the key issues of Christian faith and thought, and the Church may listen with profit to what he has to say to our later day.

FLOYD V. FILSON

Chicago
5 October, 1966

Note: Except in special cases the biblical quotations are taken by permission from the Revised Standard Version.

7

I

INTRODUCTION

FAR too much of the study devoted to the 'Letter to the Hebrews' has dealt with questions whose answer eludes us.

Who wrote it? From ancient times a tradition has ascribed it to Paul, but from earliest days there was no agreement as to authorship.[1] In the Western Church, centred in Rome, the writing was known early, for Clement of Rome, writing about AD 96, reflects knowledge of it,[2] but Pauline authorship was not accepted in the West until the fourth century.[3] Barnabas was declared to be the author by Tertullian[4]; Irenaeus, Hippolytus, and Gaius of Rome did not accept Pauline authorship; the Muratorian Canon does not include it among Paul's letters; and there are other indications of rejection of Pauline authorship in the West.

The Eastern Church tended from early times to accept Pauline authorship, but this view was not unchallenged, and when held it was subject at first to interesting qualifications. Clement of Alexandria held that Paul wrote it in Hebrew and Luke translated it into its present Greek form.[5] Origen, keenly aware of the fact that Hebrews differs from the unquestioned Pauline letters, and acquainted with views that ascribed the writing to Clement of Rome or Luke, concluded that the thoughts came from Paul, but he added that 'only God knows who actually wrote the letter'.[6]

---

[1] A detailed study of the tradition in the East and in the West is found in Franz Overbeck, *Zur Geschichte des Kanons* (Chemnitz: Ernst Schmeitzner, 1880), pp. 1–70.

[2] See e.g. the use of Hebrews 1 in *I Clem*. 36.

[3] A concise summary of data on 'Authorship' and 'Canonicity' is given by F. F. Bruce in *The Epistle to the Hebrews* (London: Marshall, Morgan and Scott, and Grand Rapids: Wm. B. Eerdmans Publishing Co., 1964), pp. xxxv–xlii, xliv–xlvii.

[4] In his work, *On Modesty* (*De pudicitia*), ch. 20. A good statement of the case for this view is given by Eduard Riggenbach, *Der Brief an die Hebräer* (Leipzig: Deichert, 1913), pp. xxxiv–xlviii.

[5] See Eusebius, *Church History*, VI.14.2–4.

[6] The relevant passages are quoted in Eusebius, *op. cit.*, VI.25.11–14.

By the end of the fourth century, Pauline authorship was generally accepted, and this remained true until the Reformation. Then
Erasmus renewed the ancient doubts. Luther conjectured that
Apollos was the author, and other prominent Reformers, Calvin
included, could not accept Paul as the author.[7] The question of
authorship continues to be discussed, but apart from the Roman
Catholic view that Paul was the author and some disciple of his the
actual writer,[8] the general view today is that Paul was not the
author.[9] A few scholars accept the tradition that Barnabas wrote
Hebrews,[10] some think that Apollos was the author,[11] but a large
number are content to say that the author is unknown.[12]

The reference to 'our brother Timothy' in 13.23 may indicate
that the author had contacts with or belonged to the wing of the
Church influenced by Paul, but the remarkable differences from
Paul in thought and style warn against making too much of this
possibility. In any case, 2.3 indicates that the author wrote at the
earliest in the second generation of the Church.

To whom was Hebrews written? It may be suggested that the
Christians addressed were Roman residents, and that their past
persecution mentioned in 10.32–34 was Nero's persecution of the
Christians at Rome about AD 64. In that case the recipients were
Roman Christians. But 12.4 states that the church addressed had
suffered no blood martyrdoms. The only clue to the location of
the Christians addressed is found in 13.24, where οἱ ἀπὸ τῆς Ἰταλίας
probably means 'those who come from Italy', Christians whose
homeland is Italy but who at the time of writing are with the
writer in some other place and send greetings back to their

[7] See Bruce, *op. cit.*, pp. xxxix–xli, xlvi–xlvii.

[8] The three decisions on this question given by the Pontifical Biblical Com-
mission on 24 June 1914 permit this distinction. See *Enchiridion Biblicum*,
2nd ed. (Rome, 1954), pp. 129–30.

[9] A prominent exception to this statement is William Leonard, *The
Authorship of the Epistle to the Hebrews* (London: Burns, Oates, and Wash-
bourne, 1939). He defends direct Pauline authorship.

[10] See Bruce, *op. cit.*, note 62 on p. xxxvii.

[11] See especially C. Spicq, *L'Épître aux Hébreux* (Paris: G. Gabalda et Cie,
1952), Vol. I, pp. 197–219, and T. W. Manson, *Studies in the Gospels and
Epistles* (Manchester: University Press, and Philadelphia: Westminster Press,
1962), who proposes to call it 'the Epistle of Apollos to the Churches of the
Lycus Valley' (p. 242).

[12] So William Manson, *The Epistle to the Hebrews* (London: Hodder and
Stoughton, 1951), pp. 169–72; and Werner Georg Kümmel, *Introduction to the
New Testament*, Eng. translation by A. J. Mattill, Jr. (Nashville: Abingdon
Press, and London: SCM Press, 1965), pp. 281–2.

Christian comrades in Italy.[13] In this case the church or church groups addressed most likely were located in the city of Rome. But possibly the words mean 'those here with me in Italy' send greetings to 'you' (the recipients) in some other unnamed place.[14] In this case we can say nothing definite concerning the place of residence of the recipients of Hebrews.[15]

Where was Hebrews written? As just noted, the place of writing was just possibly Rome or some other place in Italy, but probably was some other city whose identity eludes us.

When was Hebrews written? It often has been argued that it must have been written before the fall of Jerusalem in AD 70, since after that date the writer would surely have pointed to the fall of Jerusalem to support his case. It has been contended that this event, which included the destruction of the Temple and the cessation of the Jewish sacrifices there offered, would inevitably have been mentioned by the author of Hebrews, if he wrote after AD 70; he would have used that event as proof that God had set aside the outmoded Jewish sacrificial system. But it has rightly been noted that the writer discusses the Jewish sacrificial system solely on the basis of the Old Testament Scripture and the wilderness 'Tent' or tabernacle there described. He does not refer to the Jerusalem temple. It would therefore go too far to say that the writer of Hebrews would have been bound to refer to the destruction of Jerusalem and the Jewish Temple had he written after AD 70. The date of the writing of Hebrews cannot be determined with certainty; it could be before AD 70, but it could with some reason be set not long before AD 95.[16]

[13] See Kümmel, *op. cit.*, p. 281.

[14] Theodore H. Robinson, *The Epistle to the Hebrews* (Moffatt New Testament Commentary; London: Hodder and Stoughton, 1933), p. 206, translates the phrase as 'the Christians of Italy'. The issue can be left undecided, as is done in the New English Bible: 'Greetings to you from our Italian friends.'

[15] For the view that Hebrews was sent to 'a "Hebrew" minority' in the church at Rome see W. Manson, *op. cit.*, p. 183; for Alexandria as the destination see S. G. F. Brandon, *The Fall of Jerusalem and the Christian Church* (London: SPCK, 1951), pp. 239–40. Jerusalem also has been proposed as the destination by Wm. Leonard (*op. cit.*, p. 43). Arnold Ehrhardt, *The Framework of the New Testament Stories* (Manchester: University Press, and Cambridge, Mass.: Harvard University Press, 1964), p. 109, says Hebrews was 'a message of consolation from the Church at Rome to Christians in the Holy Land after the fall of Jerusalem'.

[16] For a study of the problems concerning the date and an argument for the date AD 67, see Spicq, *op. cit.*, Vol. I, pp. 253–61. Hugh Montefiore, in *The Epistle to the Hebrews* (London: A. and C. Black, and New York: Harper

It is unfortunate that so much attention has been paid to questions of authorship, destination, place of writing and date. No adequate evidence is available to support a definite and dependable answer. The frustratingly inconclusive study of Hebrews should make it clear that we cannot find certain answers to the questions: Who? To whom? From where? When?

In such a situation the one promising line of study open to us is an intensive examination of the writing itself. The author of Hebrews was admittedly a careful and competent writer. His own words can tell us much about himself, his purpose, and the situation of the people he addressed.

The present study proceeds in a way which to our knowledge has not been used before. Its primary focus is on the more informal and personal material of chapter 13. This concluding chapter presents critical questions which demand discussion. At the same time, it contains statements and insights of great importance for the understanding of the entire writing. We first attempt, in ch. 2, to throw new light on the form and function of chapter 13, and then in ch. 3 proceed to show by an examination of the main themes of chapter 13 how far this concluding section is vitally linked with the preceding chapters 1–12.

---

and Row, 1964), p. 12, dates Hebrews between AD 52 and 54, and holds that Apollos wrote it.

2

THE FORM AND FUNCTION OF CHAPTER 13

I. UNIQUE ASPECTS OF THIS CHAPTER

THE reader of Hebrews cannot fail to sense a change of tone and content when he passes from the close of chapter 12 to the beginning of chapter 13. Up to that point the argument has been closely knit and carefully developed. Jesus Christ the divine Son is the unique High Priest whose once-for-all unique and sufficient priestly sacrifice, followed by his continual priestly intercession, provides the full answer to the spiritual needs of men. The exhortation to take full advantage of this divinely provided way of salvation and to live faithfully in obedience to the Lord is matched by the urgent warning not to fall away from so great a privilege, 'for our God is a consuming fire' (12.29).

The unity of these twelve chapters is clear. It is possible—though not probable—that in developing his argument in such discussions as 1.5–13 and 2.6–13 the author of Hebrews used an already existing 'Testimony Book', a collection of related and particularly useful Scripture passages.[1] It may be—though it need not be so—that in the exposition and application of certain Old Testament passages, namely, Ps. 2.7 (quoted in 5.5); Ps. 40.6–8 (in 10.5–7); Ps. 95.7–11 (in 3.7–11); Ps. 110.4 (in 5.6), and Jer. 31.31–34 (in 8.8–12), and also in the extended discussion of faith in chapter 11, the author of Hebrews made use of biblical expositions which he had previously developed and had used in his teaching prior to the writing of Hebrews itself. But to whatever oral sources or earlier literary stages the author may have been indebted, the result is his own well-knit discussion, and there is no reason to question its basic unity or the sincere urgency of its appeal.[2]

[1] C. H. Dodd presents a somewhat less rigid view in *According to the Scriptures* (London: Nisbet, 1952; New York: Charles Scribner's Sons, 1953). Note especially pp. 126–7. He thinks not of 'isolated proof-texts' but of 'certain large sections' which were 'understood as wholes'.

[2] The long discussion on faith in chapter 11 is in many ways unlike the

The change of tone at 13.1 is unmistakable. The crisis atmosphere is no longer felt. The urgent exhortation to hold fast to the faith in a crisis situation has suddenly given way to a varied series of imperatives, which present a wide range of pastoral instruction. Nearly twenty imperatives or exhortations occur in chapter 13; they deal with some fifteen separate topics. In general, the tone is one of varied pastoral counsel; it is not that of a life-and-death crisis which limits attention to one crucial concern. None of the items treated is discussed at length.

Another feature in this final chapter is the series of personal notes. They give information concerning the writer and also concerning his understanding of the situation in which the recipients and others in the Church now find themselves. Nothing quite like this had occurred in previous chapters; an earlier persecution of the Christians addressed and their need to stand fast in the critical present had beeen mentioned (10.32–39), but chapters 1–12 contain no such news items as we find in chapter 13.

An unexpected intrusion into this series of varied instructions and personal notes is 13.20–21. It is one of the most elaborate and stately benedictions to be found in the closing section of any New Testament 'letter'. This formal benediction might be expected to conclude the author's work; it seems eminently fitted to serve as such a conclusion.

But 13.20–21 is not the end of Hebrews. After the series of various commands and personal notes (13.1–19) and the formal benediction (13.20–21) come still further personal instructions and information (13.22–24), and then we find in 13.25 a second but much shorter benediction: 'Grace be with all of you.'[3]

Thus with the beginning of chapter 13 the tone and content change. We now have a calmer tone, a more varied range of topics, a brief reference to each topic rather than an extensive

literary pattern of the preceding chapters and may be an earlier formulation by the author, adapted perhaps for its use in Hebrews. But in any case the chapter continues well the thought of the author and can be understood as originally composed when Hebrews was being written.

[3] The 'Amen' which closes Hebrews in most Greek manuscripts is omitted in some of the best early textual evidence and probably was not present in the original manuscript. For a quite recent listing of the most significant evidence see *The Greek New Testament*, ed. Kurt Aland, Matthew Black, Bruce M. Metzger, and Allen Wikgren, published by five Bible Societies, 1966, p. 778. The 'Amen' is much more likely to have been added than dropped.

development of one theme, and a series of personal remarks about
the writer and recipients and others of the Church at large. We
then have a formal benediction followed by further personal items
and a brief closing benediction. How can we explain the literary
form of this final section of Hebrews? What is the function of this
section? What is its relation to chapters 1–12?

2. IS CHAPTER 13 AN INTEGRAL PART OF HEBREWS?

Once we face clearly the different content, tone, and form of this
chapter, we are not surprised that some scholars have challenged
its authenticity. The question has been raised whether chapter 13
is in whole or in part an addition to the original writing.

E. D. Jones, in an article on 'The Authorship of Hebrews
xiii',[4] made the improbable claim that Hebrews 13 was the closing
part of Paul's 'severe letter' to Corinth. Jean Héring regarded
chapter 13.1–21 as a letter which the writer of the original homily
(chapters 1–12) added when he sent a copy of his work to a
specific local church. 13.22–25, Héring thought, may have been
added by another hand, perhaps by Paul if Apollos wrote the rest
of Hebrews in the sixties.[5]

Other scholars have considered only a part of chapter 13 to be
an addition to the original work. C. C. Torrey, for example, considered 13.8–15 to be a later addition.[6] More than one scholar has
been led by the formal benediction in 13.20–21 and by the 'postscript' character of 13.22–25 to conjecture that these four closing
verses of chapter 13 were added to the original work, which ended
with 13.20–21. The view of Héring was noted in the previous
paragraph. F. J. Badcock regarded 13.23–25 as a postscript added
by Paul to a letter that was 'the voice of Barnabas' by 'the hand of
Luke'.[7] A. Vanhoye, who claimed to find in Hebrews a carefully
constructed chiastic structure, repeatedly woven together by key
words which occur at the beginning of a subdivision and then
appear again at or very near to the close of the section, found that
his theory could not include 13.19 or 13.22–25 in its neat chiastic

[4] In *The Expository Times* 46 (1934–5), pp. 562–7.
[5] *L'Épître aux Hébreux* (Neuchatel: Delachaux et Niestlé, 1954), pp. 121–7.
[6] 'The Authorship and Character of the So-called Epistle to the Hebrews',
Journal of Biblical Literature, 30 (1911), pp. 137–56.
[7] *The Pauline Epistles and the Epistle to the Hebrews in Their Historical Setting*
(London: SPCK, 1937), p. 198.

structure. He conjectured that these verses were added to the original work when it was being sent to a particular church.[8]

W. Wrede[9] noted a difference between the earlier chapters of the writing and the closing chapter 13. He conjectured that the writer set out to produce a formal treatise, but as he came to the close of his work he decided to give it the appearance of a letter by Paul; he did not revise the earlier part of his writing to conform to this altered purpose, but contented himself with making the ending hint at the Pauline authorship which he hoped would give acceptance and influence to his writing.

None of these critical views has won any wide acceptance. In fact, it is a little surprising, in view of the decidedly different tone and content of chapter 13, that so few scholars have felt driven to such hypotheses. The steadily dominant view that Hebrews can best be explained as a literary unity is represented by the strong arguments for unity by R. V. G. Tasker[10] and C. Spicq.[11]

To support such a conclusion and add fresh reasons for regarding Hebrews 13 as an original and integral part of the writing, we must first survey the varied views as to the literary form of Hebrews. Against that background we can show how chapter 13 fits effectively into the form used.

3. THE LITERARY FORM OF HEBREWS

The difficulty in identifying the literary form of Hebrews is that none of the terms we use to describe modern types of literary works fits exactly the form and nature of Hebrews. We naturally try to describe such a writing by one English word. But in so doing we are inevitably led to use an inexact term, and so we conceal to some degree the actual nature of the writing we are studying. It will further our study if we list the chief terms used to describe the literary nature of Hebrews and note the truth and the misleading implications of each term.[12]

---

[8] *La Structure Littéraire de l'Épître aux Hébreux* (Paris: Desclée de Brouwer, 1963), pp. 219–21.

[9] In *Das literarische Rätsel des Hebräerbriefs* (Göttingen: Vandenhoeck and Ruprecht, 1906).

[10] 'The Integrity of the Epistle to the Hebrews', in *The Expository Times*, 47 (1935–6), pp. 136–8.

[11] 'L'Authenticité du chapitre XIII de l'Épître aux Hébreux', in *Coniectanea Neotestamentica*, 11 (1947), pp. 226–36.

[12] On the literary form of Hebrews see Otto Michel, *Der Brief an die*

(i) Hebrews has been called an essay or treatise.[13] These terms point to the serious, orderly, scholarly treatment of a theme, and to some extent Hebrews fits this description. But they fail in at least two respects to represent the nature and literary form of this writing. For one thing, a treatise or essay is a general discussion of some aspect of truth and life, but Hebrews was directed to a definite group of Christians and concerned their urgent life situation. It was to be read aloud to that group to help it meet its crisis.

Moreover, a treatise or essay is content-centred; it aims to clarify truth. But Hebrews is marked by repeated and urgent exhortation directed to the special group addressed. This personal focus and this hortatory tone are not adequately expressed by such terms as treatise or essay. The author's main attention is directed to the life situation of the people addressed. The concern of the writer is to guide those addressed to act loyally and responsibly in the face of that situation.

(ii) The word oration has been used, though rarely, to describe Hebrews.[14] This term takes account of the fact that Hebrews was written to be read aloud to a definite group of Christians. But in itself the word oration fails to express the basic fact that this writing was prepared to be read to a group from whom the writer is separated at the time. The written document is to some extent a substitute for an oral message directly spoken to the people whom the author would like to address in person. Someone else must read this writing to the people addressed. The word oration does not express this fact.

(iii) Hebrews has often been called a sermon or homily.[15] In many ways this term is useful and accurate. It expresses the per-

---

Hebräer (Göttingen: Vandenhoeck and Ruprecht, 1949), pp. 1–9; C. Spicq, *L'Épître aux Hébreux*, Vol. I, pp. 4–26; Kümmel, *op. cit.*, pp. 276–9. The question concerning the literary form of Hebrews is discussed in several passages of Adolf Deissmann, *Light From the Ancient East*, translated by Lionel R. M. Strachan, 4th ed. (London: Hodder and Stoughton, and New York: Geo. H. Doran Co., 1927); see p. 243.

[13] Wrede, *op. cit.*, p. 14, calls chapters 1–12 '*abhandlungsmässig*' in content and form.

[14] C. C. Torrey, *op. cit.*, p. 146, uses the word 'oration'. But he later uses other designation, such as 'a sermon transformed into an epistle' and 'anonymous sermon'.

[15] See the discussion of Michel, *op. cit.*, p. 5, who uses but develops and corrects the earlier (1797) description of Hebrews by J. Berger as a sermon.

sonal concern of the writer for the spiritual welfare and faithful integrity of the people addressed. It indicates that this is a biblically-based Christian message which has an assembled congregation in mind (or, if it is to be read to more than one congregation in the city of its destination, it has all of these assembled congregations in mind). In a sermon or homily the note of exhortation, of urgent appeal, is inevitably present, as it is in Hebrews.

Yet in at least two respects the word sermon or homily is not a correct and adequate description of Hebrews. In the first place, a sermon properly speaking is the direct personal statement of Christian truth and the exhortation to the hearers to heed this truth. It is of the essence of a sermon that the preacher faces his congregation and speaks in person what he believes is the urgent word of God to them at the time. But Hebrews is sent from a distance to be read to a congregation in the absence of the author.

Moreover, the widely ranging general imperatives in chapter 13 are not what we expect in a sermon, which normally comes to a conclusion and climax in the clear statement and application of the aspect of truth on which the sermon centres. One does not expect a sermon to conclude with a miscellaneous medley of commands, personal information, and general instructions. Hebrews is something more than and different from a sermon or homily.

(iv) Emphasis is often placed on the fact that Hebrews consists largely of biblical exposition.[16] It is true that a considerable portion of the whole work cites and applies Old Testament passages in the wording found in the Greek Old Testament. The clear assumption of the writer is that the Old Testament foreshadows and finds its fulfilment in the coming and work of Jesus Christ, the divine Son and one effective high priest. The concentration on the scriptural basis of the gospel message is so strong that the discussion of the high priest and the sanctuary deals entirely with the Tent in the wilderness as described in the Pentateuch; it does not deal at all with the Temple in Jerusalem and the high priests who ministered there.

The fact remains, however, that the basic literary form of Hebrews is not biblical exposition. Substantial portions of the writing may be so described, but they use the Scripture to throw

---

[16] On the use of the Old Testament in Hebrews see C. Spicq, *L'Épître aux Hébreux*, Vol. I, pp. 330–50.

light on the person and work of Jesus Christ, and a significant portion of Hebrews is not cast in the form of biblical exposition. This is true especially of the extensive sections given over to exhortation of the recipients to be faithful and loyal to their confession (2.1–4; 3.7–4.13; 4.14–16; 5.11–6.12; 10.19–39; 12.1–29). The biblical exposition gives the background and basis for such repeated exhortations, but such exposition is not the author's basic interest and purpose.

Moreover, chapter 13, with which we are particularly concerned, makes little use of biblical exposition. Only 13.6, with its quotation of Ps. 118.6, recalls the biblical background of the writer's thinking and argument. It is quite inadequate to describe Hebrews as biblical exposition.

(v) The most frequently used term to describe Hebrews is epistle or letter.[17] It contains essential truth. The Greek word 'epistle', ἐπιστολή, means a writing sent from a distance to convey a message which the writer is not present to deliver directly by word of mouth. It reflects a living relationship between writer and recipient(s) and implies a specific situation of sufficient importance to move the writer to send his message so as to make it known to the recipients as soon as possible. It expresses much of the truth to say that Hebrews is a letter.

Nevertheless, this statement needs to be qualified. It is not a private personal letter, but is intended to be read to a group of Christians met together for worship and consideration of their critical situation. It is intended to be a significant part of a service of fellowship and worship. It therefore lacks something of the informal atmosphere normally found in a personal letter from a friend. Furthermore, the writer assumes without discussion that he has such a relation to the Christians addressed that he can speak sternly to them with a note of authority. His writing is not just a friendly letter from an equal. Written to play a prominent

[17] On the letter in ancient times see the article on 'Letter' by O. J. F. Seitz in *The Interpreter's Dictionary of the Bible* (New York: Abingdon Press, 1962), Vol. III K-Q, pp. 113–15. Seitz does not discuss the view of Otto Roller, who in *Das Formular der paulinischen Briefe* (Stuttgart: W. Kohlhammer Verlag, 1933), pp. 237, 620–6, argues that the lack of the opening address and closing greeting marks the Western Asiatic as opposed to the Greek type of letter; in the Western Asiatic type the bearer of the letter delivered the address and closing personal greeting orally. I John he sees as a pure Western Asiatic type, and Hebrews as a mixed type, being Western Asiatic in its lack of an opening address and Greek in its benediction at the end.

part in a service of worship and fellowship, and written with a tacit assumption of authority, the writing is something more than a private informal letter.

Many years ago Adolf Deissmann, impressed by the numerous letters found among the ancient papyri discovered in Egypt, made a distinction between a letter, an informal personal communication, and an epistle, written with a more formal note and intended for public reading or for reading as a form of literature.[18] There is such a distinction as Deissmann pointed out. But the use which Deissmann made of this distinction was that many of our New Testament letters are real letters and not literary epistles. To a degree Deissmann's distinction is well founded. The New Testament writers of letters were not seeking literary recognition. They did not write their letters for publication. In almost all cases they wrote to meet the needs of a local church or a group of churches; they wrote to speak to current situations and to meet present needs.

But every New Testament letter is much more than a private personal letter.[19] Each was written to be read to a group of Christians gathered together for fellowship, worship, and consideration of their situation and duty. The note of authority with which Paul wrote cannot be ignored, even in letters which traditionally are considered personal letters. Philemon was sent not merely to Philemon, but also to Apphia and Archippus 'and the church in your house' (Philemon 2). Each of the Pastoral Letters, whatever their authorship, was written to the Church in a rather general way; the word 'you' in the closing prayer asking God's grace for the recipient(s) is in the plural number (I Tim. 6.21; II Tim. 4.22; Titus 3.15).[20] III John comes as near to being a personal letter as any letter in the New Testament, but even in this brief letter a more than private use of the letter is probably taken for granted (cf. III John 15: 'Greet the friends, every one of them').

These observations help us to see that Hebrews with its somewhat formal attitude to the Christians addressed and its rather formal literary structure in the first twelve chapters of the writing

[18] On this distinction and its application to Hebrews see Deissmann, *op. cit.*, pp. 228–44.
[19] This is quite generally recognized now by New Testament scholars.
[20] See for the textual evidence on I Tim. 6.21 *The Greek New Testament*, ed. Kurt Aland, Matthew Black, Bruce M. Metzger, and Allen Wikgren, p. 730.

is not so radically different from the other New Testament 'letters' as is sometimes thought. In a sense it may be called a letter, for it was a written message sent to a church (or possibly to a local group of churches) to be read to its assembly, but it is a quite formal kind of letter, and only in the closing section of the writing does the personal relation of the writer to the recipients emerge clearly and in a somewhat more informal way.

(vi) Hebrews may be called an exhortation ($\pi\alpha\rho\acute{\alpha}\kappa\lambda\eta\sigma\iota\varsigma$). Indeed, this is what the writer himself calls it, a 'word of exhortation' (13.22).[21] Large portions of the writing fit this description perfectly (2.1–4; 3.7–4.13; 4.14–16; 5.11–6.12; 10.19–39; 12.1–29; and the frequent imperatives and exhortations of chapter 13).

The writer obviously has no interest in theological discussion for its own sake. He is concerned to give the recipients a right view of Jesus Christ and his saving work, in order to show how great a privilege the recipients have and what an immense and irreparable loss they would suffer if they let the passage of time, the hardships of discipleship, or the lure of any other loyalty rob them of their joy in faith and faithfulness in life. We understand Hebrews rightly only if we keep this urgent note of exhortation clearly before us in all our discussion of the form and meaning of the writing.

How then can we best describe the literary form represented by Hebrews? If it is true, as we have contended, that no one English word will clearly and accurately express what kind of literary form Hebrews embodies, then we must state our answer in the form of a sentence which successively focuses on a series of points, each of which is an integral part of the full answer.

A tentative answer would be as follows: Hebrews is a written message, which sets forth vital aspects of the Christian gospel on the basis of Scripture (which to the writer was of course the Old Testament); it was sent from a distance to be read aloud to a Christian congregation assembled for worship, fellowship, and instruction; and it was the work of a leader who was known to these Christians and could speak to them concerning their current situation with a note of authority and urgent exhortation and deep pastoral concern for their total Christian life.

---

[21] This is probably the most widely accepted description of Hebrews among scholars today.

4. THE FOURFOLD STRUCTURE OF CHAPTER 13

We noted earlier the at first sight rather curious fourfold structure of chapter 13. After the carefully woven argument of chapters 1–12, focused on a right understanding of Jesus Christ the one high priest and his once-for-all and fully effective sacrifice, we suddenly encounter in chapter 13 a wide-ranging series of imperatives and exhortations which are not directly connected with the preceding discussion. We are no longer troubled by this succession of general and quite varied commands and instructions, for we have noted that the writer, out of a deep pastoral concern and in view of his necessary absence from these Christians, takes this opportunity to speak not only concerning the special problem discussed in chapters 1–12 but also concerning other points which he thinks he should mention for the good of the Christians addressed. His inclusion of these added points expresses his pastoral concern for his Christian friends and his awareness that they face more than one problem concerning which they need pastoral instruction and exhortation.

When he has called such varied instructions to their attention and has given them items of personal information, he shows by the formal benediction his awareness that he is speaking through this writing to a congregation in common worship. It expresses his prayer for the effective working of God in them as they respond faithfully to God's gifts by a life of fruitful helpfulness. But though this would seem to be the fitting place to close the writing, the sense of separation from the recipients and the sense of oneness with them in a common bond of faith and Christian concern leads him to add brief personal words before he finally closes his writing by a shorter benediction which puts all their personal relations and problems under the needed grace of God.

This fourfold pattern for the closing part of a written message —(1) varied teaching, injunctions, and information; (2) formal benediction; (3) personal greetings and messages; and (4) closing brief benediction—may not be the way we would close such a writing to Christian friends. But before we conclude that the writer of Hebrews was a blundering composer who could not follow accepted patterns of communication to Christian churches there is a highly important point to note about this fourfold structure. Its use here is not unique in early Christian 'letters'. Or the contrary, it is a pattern to which we find several parallels in the New Testament. Once we clearly see this, we shall not be tempted to belittle the literary ability of the writer or think that chapter 13 must have been written by another person than the author of chapters 1–12.

Let us note briefly other New Testament examples of this fourfold structure:

(i) *I Thessalonians*. (*a*) In 5.12–22 we find a compact series of instructions concerning Christian duty in a variety of life situations. (*b*) Then follows in 5.23–24 a formal benediction and an assurance of God's faithfulness. (*c*) This is followed in 5.25–27 by a request for prayer for Paul, a concise greeting to all, and instruction that the letter be read to all the Thessalonian Christians. (*d*) Then the writing concludes in 5.28 with a shorter benediction than the formal one we found in 5.23–24.

(ii) *II Thessalonians*. (*a*) A section of instructions and warnings closes with 3.15. (*b*) Then 3.16 expresses an earnest prayer that the Thessalonian Christians may be blessed with the peace and presence of God. (*c*) Paul then takes the pen to add in 3.17 a personal greeting whose handwriting will identify any letter from him. (*d*) Finally we have in 3.18 the fourth part of the fourfold structure, the brief benediction praying that God's grace may be with all the Thessalonian brethren.

(iii) *Galatians*. (*a*) After a section of varied instructions concerning Christian living (6.1–10), Paul takes the pen to summarize in 6.11–15 the message of this letter. (*b*) Then 6.16 offers the earnest prayer that God's peace and mercy may rest upon his faithful and true Israel, the Church. But this is not the end of the letter, for (*c*) 6.17 adds personal words, and (*d*) they in turn are followed by the final benediction in 6.18.

(iv) *II Timothy*. Here again the fourfold structure appears rather clearly. (*a*) 4.9–18a contains personal information and instructions. (*b*) A doxology follows (4.18b). (*c*) Further personal information is given in 4.19–21. (*d*) Then comes a benediction in two parts, praying that God's presence and grace may be with Timothy and his companions in the churches he serves ('you' is plural here, as it is in the closing verse of Titus and probably of First Timothy).[22]

(v) *Philippians*. Here too the fourfold structure may be discerned. (*a*) 4.10–19 deals with Paul's response to the gift the

---

[22] On I Tim. 6.21 see note 20.

Philippian church has sent to him. (*b*) Then follows a doxology in 4.20. (*c*) Personal greetings are added in 4.21–22, and (*d*) the final benediction follows in 4.23.

(vi) *I Peter*. The fourfold pattern is not so clear here. But it is worth noting that (*a*) following various exhortations in 5.1–10 we find (*b*) a formal ascription of praise to God and an 'Amen' in 5.11, (*c*) personal information and greetings in 5.12–14a, and (*d*) a brief benediction in 5.14b. The key feature of the fourfold structure, a formal benediction or doxology followed by personal items and a brief closing benediction, is present.

(vii) *Romans*. It would take us too far afield to discuss in detail all the problems raised by the unusual number of benedictions found in the closing chapters of Romans. In some manuscripts the elaborate doxology usually found in 16.25–27 is found at the end of chapter 14, or at the end of chapter 15, or in two of these three locations. A short benediction is found in 15.33, in 16.20, and in the textually highly suspect 16.24.[23] Since it is often suggested that chapter 16, or most of what it now contains, was a separate letter of recommendation for Phoebe and was sent to Ephesus, and since there are indications that Romans in slightly shortened and edited forms was circulated in the ancient Church as a statement of Paul's essential message, it is difficult to know what to make of this abundance of benedictions, and we cannot be certain exactly how Paul's original Letter to the Roman Church ended.[24]

We need only say for our present purpose that this Letter too may have had the fourfold structure found at the close of several Letters, in which two benedictions formed a frequent though by no means ever-present feature of the conclusion of New Testament letters. The main letter was concluded by personal information and instructions followed by a formal benediction or doxology, and this was followed by further personal information and greetings and then by a final benediction.

In the other New Testament 'letters' just examined we find so many parallels or partial parallels to the fourfold structure of Hebrews 13 that there is no reason for suspecting the unity and integrity of Hebrews because it has this to us strange structure.

[23] For a convenient summary of the confusing textual evidence on these points see *The Greek New Testament* cited in notes 3 and 20, pp. 576 f.

[24] For a discussion of these problems concerning the Greek text of Romans, see John Knox in *The Interpreter's Bible* IX (1954), pp. 363–8.

General instructions and information not closely connected with the content of the main body of the writing were entirely in place. The first benediction showed the writer's awareness that his message would be read aloud at a meeting of the congregation(s) to which it was sent. The formal benediction was followed by personal items of various kinds. Then a second benediction brought the entire writing to a close. We need have no hesitation in accepting Hebrews 13 as an integral part of the total work.

5. THE RELATION OF CHAPTER 13 TO CHAPTERS 1–12

Once we have grasped this fourfold structure of chapter 13, we can see how to study this chapter in relation to the earlier chapters of Hebrews. Chapters 1–12 obviously have a well-knit structure of thought which we cannot expect to find in the wide-ranging pastoral concern and personal items of chapter 13. The literary and topical unity of chapters 1–12 will not be matched by the more general range of interests in chapter 13. There may be aspects of Christian thought which are carefully developed in the course of chapters 1–12 but are not found at all in chapter 13. Chapter 13 in turn may touch on Christian obligations and personal situations which there was no reason to discuss or even mention in chapters 1–12. We cannot expect to find in chapter 13 neat and complete parallels to all that chapters 1–12 present.

If, however, the same man wrote the entire work as we have it in our New Testament, we can expect to find in chapter 13 some measure of agreement with chapters 1–12 in vocabulary, style, and content.[25] To some degree the themes and outlook of chapter 13 should show similarity to the earlier chapters. We propose to test this possibility. We proceed to study the themes and concerns of chapter 13 to see how far they are paralleled in the themes and interests of chapters 1–12.

Such a study might take the form of a verse by verse examination of chapter 13, an examination concluded by a summary and interpretation of the individual items learned in such an exegetical study. It should make for greater clarity and better focus, however, to direct attention to the key themes that stand out in chapter 13 and ask in the case of each one how far it is paralleled

[25] On basic agreements in style and vocabulary, see the essay of C. Spicq cited in note 11.

in chapters 1–12. The result may be to throw new light on the earlier chapters as well as on the meaning and importance of the closing chapter of Hebrews. The parallels may be the more striking because they result from the comparative study of two quite different forms of literary expression, the close-knit discussion of the first twelve chapters and the more general and wide-ranging exhortation of chapter 13.

3

KEY THEMES OF CHAPTER 13

1. 'MY WORD OF EXHORTATION'

IN these words, as has already been noted, the author has given the most apt description that could be used to state briefly the nature and purpose of his writing. He has written to arouse, urge, encourage, and exhort the hearers of his message to realize how completely God has met their need by the work of Christ and what a priceless privilege they have thus been given.

He recognizes that in what he has said he has gone beyond 'the elementary doctrines of Christ' (6.1) and given the Christians addressed 'solid food' such as is suited 'for the mature' members of the Church (5.14). The addressees have failed thus far to attain the Christian maturity which in view of their years of discipleship should now mark their thought and conduct (5.12). But he is not content to repeat the rudimentary teachings they should long ago have mastered. He chooses rather to go on to an advanced discussion of the high priesthood of Christ and his once-for-all completely effective sacrifice for sins.

As he does this, his work could seem to be essentially a thorough theological discussion. But that would be a mistaken conception of his basic purpose. His aim is not merely intellectual and theological. He uses these aspects to sweep aside any doubts concerning the truth and crucial importance of the gospel, to make clear the completeness and adequacy of God's work in Christ, and to drive home the fact that by their acceptance or indifference these Christians will make the crucial decision which will determine their spiritual status now and for all time to come.[1] In every statement with important theological content he is urging the recipients to realize how much is at stake in their response to this gospel.

[1] Cf. Erich Grässer, in 'Der Hebräerbrief 1938–1963', *Theologische Rundschau* 30 (1964), p. 198, who quotes approvingly Käsemann's statement that in Hebrews Christology is utilized to aid exhortation.

To so basic and decisive a message mild adhesion or lukewarm allegiance is no adequate response. Nothing less is called for than grateful faith expressed in active, steady faithfulness.

But the author does not express his urgency merely by the urgent tone in which he presents the truth of the gospel. He repeatedly follows a passage of earnest theological discussion by explicit and extended exhortation to take seriously and act upon the truth he has presented. This vibrant hortatory note occurs not only in 2.1–4; 3.7–4.13; 4.14–16; 5.11–6.12; 10.19–39; and 12.1–29 but also in the greater part of chapter 13, which thus has the same dominant note as do the earlier chapters. The urgency built into the theological discussion and the repeated explicit exhortation which continually recurs in this series of exhortations cannot be disregarded. The note of exhortation is so recurrent and is expressed at such length as to be dominant in the total work.

This writing is thus the author's 'word of exhortation' to the Christians who will hear his message read to them in their assembly for common worship. His theological discussion is not an end in itself. It is only his means to reach these Christians with an urgent exhortation to hold fast to their faith, to show their faith in faithfulness, and to let no passage of time or renewal of persecution dull the stout steadfastness of their Christian confession and obedience.

There have been attempts to deny that the author himself described his work as his 'word of exhortation'. Overbeck, for example, held that 13.22–25 was a later addition, to promote the (false) idea that Paul had written the work.[2] Wrede held a similar view, but with the idea that the author included these closing words in order to suggest subtly Pauline authorship and so promote acceptance of his work as from the Apostle Paul.[3] It has also been suggested that the 'word of exhortation' referred only to chapters 1–12; in this case all of chapter 13 would be an addition to the original work.[4] Vanhoye held that these closing verses (13.19, 22–25) were a brief covering letter; the 'word of exhortation' on his view consisted only of 1.1–13.21 (less 13.19).[5]

Once we have understood the fourfold structure of chapter 13

---

[2] F. Overbeck, *op. cit.*, p. 16. [3] See ch. 2, note 9.

[4] This might be the position of those who regard chapter 13 as a supplement or covering letter, written at a time later than the earlier chapters and sent with them to some group not in mind when chapters 1–12 were composed. See ch. 2, note 5, concerning Héring's view. [5] See ch. 2, note 8.

and have come to see clearly that to follow the formal benediction of
13.20–21 with personal messages and a shorter benediction con-
forms to a well-known practice, we have no reason to feel uneasy
concerning the presence of 13.22–25 in Hebrews. In particular,
the writer's informal but apt designation of 1.1–13.21 as his 'word
of exhortation' is entirely in place and is suited to the context.

Since 'exhortation' (παράκλησις) is thus so apt a description of
Hebrews, it will be worth while to examine the word a little more
closely.[6] It goes back to the verb παρακαλέω, which means 'be-
seech', 'entreat', or 'console', 'comfort', or 'encourage', 'exhort'.
Present in all these meanings is the idea of an urgent appeal; the
various English translations reflect varying situations in the relation of the person speaking to the person(s) addressed.

The noun παράκλησις occurs in the New Testament twenty-four
times; we find it four times in Acts (4.36; 9.31; 13.15; 15.31),
seventeen times in eight Pauline letters (one is I Tim. 4.13), and
three times in Hebrews (6.18; 12.5; 13.22). The shade of meaning
in each passage calls for study, especially since our English words
used to translate it have varied in meaning from one period to
another. We can see this if we compare the English translations
in the Authorized (King James) Version (AV) with those in the
Revised Standard Version (RSV). The AV uses 'consolation'
eleven times, 'comfort' four times, 'exhortation' eight times, and
'entreaty' once. The RSV uses 'comfort' nine times (six of them
in II Cor. 1.3–7), 'encouragement' six times, 'exhortation' five
times, 'preaching' once, 'appeal' twice, and the idea of 'earnestness'
or 'earnest exhortation' once (II Cor. 8.4, where 'earnestly' more
literally translated would be 'with much earnestness'; AV has
'with much entreaty').[7]

The dominant use of 'consolation' and 'comfort' in the AV is
misleading today. These words now carry too much of a passive
note; they suggest mainly getting people to accept with resigna-
tion and submission whatever sorrow or tragedy has come to
them. In AD 1611 there was heard in these words, particularly in

[6] For a study of παρακαλέω and παράκλησις see G. Kittel, *Theologisches
Wörterbuch zum Neuen Testament* (Stuttgart: W. Kohlhammer, hereafter cited
as *TWNT*), Vol. V (1953), pp. 771–98, where the phrase in Heb. 13.22 is
translated: 'Wort des ermahnenden Zuspruchs' (p. 793).

[7] The New English Bible (NEB) translates more freely. It uses most
frequently 'exhortation' and 'encouragement'. Only in II Cor. 1.3–7 does it
use 'consolation'. It never uses 'comfort'.

'comfort', more of a note of strengthening, encouraging, and summoning the afflicted and hard pressed to live with new courage and vitality in view of the gifts, resources, and tasks which God bestows. Even 'console', as *Webster's Third New Internationa Dictionary* says of its use today, meant not only to 'alleviate the grief' but also to 'raise the spirits'. This encouraging note must be heard in the New Testament uses of the word παράκλησις; it does not exclude the place of comforting and consoling in our popular modern sense, but it subordinates that use to the more active meaning.

It would be well to avoid the translation 'comfort' and use 'encouragement' and 'exhortation', not in order to eliminate the idea of soothing 'comfort' in hardship and affliction, but to gather up this idea in the larger concept of leading Christians to respond to sorrow, hardship, and affliction with God-given strength and courage. Such strength and courage are a result of the encouragement the gospel gives and the exhortation it presents to live actively in faith that the gospel is indeed dependably true.

Certainly in Heb. 13.22 the noun παράκλησις means the author's 'exhortation' to believe and stake all on the truth of the gospel as he has set it forth. It is an exhortation that throbs with 'encouragement' (though also with stern warning) and with earnest 'appeal'.

Into such a 'word of exhortation' chapter 13 fits well. It contains a series of imperatives, urgent exhortations, and statements of personal concern for the Christians addressed. Its content and hortatory tone are in healthy harmony with the courageous and encouraging attitude which the author has taken in the preceding twelve chapters of Hebrews.

2. 'YESTERDAY'

Perhaps no word expresses the thought framework of Hebrews so well as does 'yesterday' (ἐχθές); no word serves better to prevent a false understanding of the author's viewpoint.[8] This word

[8] It is curious, and disappointing, that *TWNT* does not include a study of ἐχθές. The editors apparently saw no theological significance in its use in 13.8 William F. Arndt and F. Wilbur Gingrich, in *A Greek-English Lexicon of the New Testament and Other Early Christian Literature* (Cambridge: The University Press, 1957), a 'translation and adaptation' of Walter Bauer's great work, take ἐχθές with σήμερον to mean 'the present'. This in effect gives no meaning at all to ἐχθές.

occurs in 13.8, and in the RSV this verse is translated: 'Jesus
Christ is the same yesterday and today and for ever.' More literally
the Greek may be translated: 'Jesus Christ yesterday and today the
same and into the ages.' At first sight this verse seems to stand
alone, lacking any thought connection with either v. 7 or v. 9.
But this impression is misleading.

Verse 7 has spoken of the former leaders of the Christians
addressed. They were exemplary not only in preaching the gospel
but in their faithfulness (in Hebrews the word 'faith' includes a
strong note of faithfulness). Their faithfulness was maintained to
their death, to which the author refers when he speaks of 'the
outcome' of their life. The recipients of Hebrews, when they
think of the faithfulness of their pioneer leaders, should be en-
couraged to maintain a like faithfulness, even if, after their earlier
hardship, they must again suffer persecution.

But the reason for such faithfulness is not merely that they
should imitate the steadfastly loyal life of their former leaders.
They can and should look constantly to Jesus Christ, 'the pioneer
and perfecter of our faith' (12.2). He is the supreme example of
faithfulness and constancy, 'the same yesterday and today and for
ever'. If they keep clearly in view the unswerving loyalty and
steadfastness of Jesus Christ, they will 'not be led away by diverse
and strange teachings' such as v. 9 warns against. Verse 8 is thus
not an isolated and unconnected remark; it connects with both
what precedes and what follows.

But our point here is more general. This verse is notably suited
to serve as a true guidepost to the viewpoint of Hebrews. In
particular, the word 'yesterday', properly understood, summarizes
and points to the distinctive viewpoint and message of the author.
It points to the view that lies behind and finds frequent expression
in chapters 1–12.

This view has at times been missed, particularly by interpreters
who have been misled by a wrong use of the words 'the same'.
Under the influence of this phrase, it has sometimes been thought
that 13.8 is emphasizing the unchanging nature of Jesus Christ.
This seems to many Christians a most reasonable interpretation,
for if Jesus Christ is truly and fully divine, he would not be
expected to be subject to change; God, as the Westminster
Shorter Catechism confesses, in the answer to Question 4, is
'unchangeable'.

To this argument from the unchangeable nature of God is often added, usually more unconsciously than by conscious decision, the assumption that reality is timeless. Created things have no permanent existence; they may and will change and pass away. But what is true and real and ultimate belongs to that timeless realm which alone has primary significance. As a result of this viewpoint many interpreters of Hebrews find a dominantly Platonic note in Hebrews, and the phrase 'the same' is to them a reference to the timeless and so ultimately real significance of Jesus Christ.

This puts before us a basic question. What for the writer of Hebrews was the nature of ultimate reality? Was it time with its sequence of historical events as the key to a sound understanding of life? Or was it space as a symbol of two realms of life, one of which—and that a secondary one—was this earthly time-bound order, while the other—and that the truly significant one—was the transcendent order? In the centuries of New Testament interpretation there has been a persistent tendency to regard the writer of Hebrews as essentially Platonic in his outlook and thought. To him, it is often supposed, time with its sequence of events is not the proper or adequate form in which to state the essential Christian gospel.[9]

But 13.8 does not embody a basically Platonic point of view. The key word that points away from an essentially Platonic, basically timeless manner of thought is 'yesterday'. To be sure, if as has been suggested we were to take this word to refer to all previous time and so to mean 'from all eternity', the ideas of time and change would not be dominant. But 'yesterday' does not mean 'from all eternity' or 'throughout all the vast vistas of preceding time'.[10] It points to Jesus Christ as one who just recently became what he now is and what he always will be in all the endless succession of future ages.

[9] See the discussion of this issue by J. Cambier in A. Robert and A. Feuillet, *Introduction to the New Testament*, Eng. trs. (New York: Desclee, 1965), pp. 530–2, and Cambier's article cited on p. 531. There is truth in his view, but our argument is that whatever can be said of an always existing and never changing aspect (of God most of all), we human beings never escape the time framework in either life or thought, and the basic gospel is irrevocably expressed in time language.

[10] It is so taken, however, by Hugh Montefiore, *The Epistle to the Hebrews*, p. 242. He says that *'yesterday, today and for ever* is a graphic way of alluding to past, present and future in order to affirm the unchanging nature of Christ'.

This does not imply that quite recently Jesus Christ became completely other than what he had been before. He was and is and will remain the divine Son. But he was not until recently the qualified high priest who could make the once-for-all and fully effective sacrifice.

This may seem to us a shocking statement, but it is basic to a true understanding of Hebrews, whose author asserts it with unmistakable clarity: Christ '*learned* obedience through what he suffered; and *being made perfect* he became the source of eternal salvation to all who obey him' (5.8–9). To offer the perfect sacrifice he had to be the perfect high priest. To be the qualified perfect high priest he had to learn obedience through suffering in his earthly life. To achieve this he necessarily 'for a little while was made lower than the angels' (2.9) and 'had to be made like his brethren in every respect, so that he might become a merciful and faithful high priest in the service of God, to make expiation for the sins of his people' (2.17–18).

Amazing as the idea may seem to men, God had to 'make the pioneer of their salvation perfect through suffering' (2.10). To enter the true and heavenly sanctuary, to offer there the one perfect sacrifice on our behalf (9.11–14), and to intercede there for his people (7.25), Jesus had to *become* qualified, to be perfected, to learn obedience through what he suffered, to present his own blood as the perfect sacrifice, and then to reign with God (1.3) and continue his high priestly ministry by his intercession for his people (7.25).

All this, the author attests, has taken place. It has taken place 'in these last days' (1.2), and while the author is conscious of belonging to at least the second generation of Christians (2.3; 13.7), this does not prevent him, as he sees the coming and work of Christ in the long sweep of God's dealings with Israel, from speaking of these decisive events as having occurred 'yesterday'.

In this drama of redemption time is real; it is the setting for the saving work of Christ. And specific unique events are decisive. It was in crucial divine acts of God that salvation was won and made available. This gospel has to be stated in terms of time, in terms of one decisive network of historical events.

Nothing like it—except by way of a type or foreshadowing of that unique and fully effective climactic working of God in Christ —had been seen or done before. Nothing to rival it can ever be

Y C

expected again, for the work of Christ is complete and fully adequate and will never need to be done again. No new change in Jesus Christ will be expected or needed, for he has been 'made perfect' (5.9). So Jesus Christ is 'the same' 'today' as he became 'yesterday', and he will remain 'the same' on into the endless ages to come, 'for ever'.

This sense of the decisive and permanent effect of a unique recent historical event the author expresses by the use of two synonymous adverbs, 'once' (ἅπαξ) and 'once for all' (ἐφάπαξ). Jesus offered a fully effective sacrifice for the sins of his people 'once for all when he offered up himself' (7.27). 'He has appeared once for all at the end of the age to put away sin by the sacrifice of himself' (9.26). 'He entered once for all into the Holy Place, . . . thus securing an eternal redemption' (9.12). 'We have been sanctified through the offering of the body of Jesus Christ once for all' (10.10).

It is essentially to this radical once-only action to deal with human sin that the author refers when he speaks of 'yesterday' with its continuing effects. It was an action which deeply affected Christ, in a way that had lasting results, so that he can now be described as 'the same yesterday and today and for ever'. Thus a time sense, the sense of a unique recent decisive event, runs through the discussion in Hebrews, and what 13.8 says is a compact reference to what chapters 1–12 present in much greater detail.

To many Christians this entire discussion may seem theologically disturbing. It may seem to question the solid everlasting faithfulness and dependability of God. And it can be pointed out that Hebrews itself clearly indicates that the work of Jesus Christ continued, climaxed, and perfected what God had already spoken and done for Israel. A providential line connects the Old Testament history with the work of God in Christ (even though the author's concern for interpreting the Old Testament Scriptures, mainly the Levitical law, looms larger than his interest in the sequence of historical events in the Old Testament story). But to the author of Hebrews that history was a real history and God was at work in it. When this fact is faced and frankly considered, we must say that time is real to the author of Hebrews, and indeed we must go a step further and say that in his view time was real to God. He knew God by what God had done and said in successive events. He saw God in the ongoing time sequence, and supremely in what God had done in Jesus Christ 'yesterday'.[11]

3. 'JESUS CHRIST'

Before attempting to state in any detail how the author of Hebrews thought of Jesus, it was necessary to point out how decisive for this author was the historical understanding behind the word 'yesterday'. In that discussion it became clear that the decisive historical event of which Hebrews speaks centred in a person, Jesus Christ. It now is necessary to study more closely the identity and work of that person.

It becomes clear at once that chapter 13 does not parallel all the titles of Jesus and all the descriptions of his work which appear in chapters 1–12. But this could not be expected. Chapters 1–12 present the person and work of Jesus as the basis for the author's effective 'word of exhortation' (13.22). Chapter 13, as we saw when we made clear its fourfold structure, is largely given over to a wide-ranging list of general exhortations and personal messages. It could not be expected to repeat all that chapters 1–12 have said about Jesus and his work. But if we first survey the titles used of Jesus in chapters 1–12 and then ask how far the references in chapter 13 parallel that picture, we shall find as wide a range of agreement as we have any right to expect.

(i) *Jesus*. One fact should be noted at the outset. The author does not use Melchizedek as a name for Jesus. He calls Jesus a high priest 'after the order of Melchizedek' (5.6, 10; etc.) and 'in the likeness of Melchizedek' (7.15), but he does not use Melchizedek as a name or title of Jesus. And although his method of using Scripture might lead us to expect him to call Jesus 'King of Righteousness' and 'King of Peace' (7.3), he never does so. It is not Melchizedek's position as king but his priestly position and role which interests the author; the superiority of the priestly

---

[11] If it should be suggested that the above argument puts too much of a load on one word, it must be replied that it is precisely the word that sums up the message of Hebrews that 'in these last days' God has acted decisively with everlasting effect, and that he has so acted in Christ, who only in this quite recent time, these recent 'days of his flesh' (5.7), 'learned obedience', was 'made perfect' (5.8–9), and 'offered for all time a single sacrifice for sins' (10.12). *After* those decisive recent developments he was, is now, and always will be 'the same'.

ministry of Jesus as compared with the ministry of the Levitical priesthood is the point he draws from Melchizedek's superiority to Abraham (7.4–10).

Another fact worth notice is that the author does not find significance in the root meaning of the name and titles of Jesus. The word Jesus is the Greek form of the Hebrew name Joshua and means 'Yah(weh) is salvation' or 'Yah(weh) saves'. The writer of Matt. 1.21 was aware of that meaning when he ascribed to an angel the words, 'You shall call his name Jesus, for he will *save* his people form their sins.' The author of Hebrews either did not know the root meaning of the Hebrew name or chose to make no use of it. He never uses the title Saviour or Redeemer of Jesus. He thinks of Jesus as the historical person who acted decisively for God to make 'purification for sins' and provide 'eternal salvation' (1.3; 5.9), but he does not draw this conclusion from the root meaning of the name.

Similarly there is no evidence that he knew and used the root meaning of the word Christ. It comes from the verb χρίω, meaning 'anoint', so that Christ, Χριστός, means 'anointed'. The author uses the verb χρίω once (1.9), but he does not connect it with the messianic meaning it had in the early Apostolic Age; he speaks in 1.9 of the divine Son, whom God 'has *anointed* . . . with the oil of gladness beyond thy comrades', that is, God has anointed or endowed the Son with a higher degree of joy and bliss than is enjoyed by his comrades, whether angels or men. There is no indication that in his rather frequent use of the word Christ the author thought of the word's root meaning or of its earlier messianic reference. To him the word Christ was no longer an adjective or title but had become a proper name, especially in the thrice used double name 'Jesus Christ' (10.10; 13.8, 21).

A third general remark is that the titles used of Jesus are not mutually exclusive. The author does not use one title for one period of Jesus' work while using another title of another period. The titles overlap in their range of reference. This will become clear as we now survey the chief ways in which the author of Hebrews designates or describes Jesus.[12]

The basic function of the name Jesus is to designate the central

[12] On the person (and titles) of Jesus see Spicq, *L'Épître aux Hébreux* Vol. I, pp. 287–301; B. F. Westcott, *The Epistle to the Hebrews*, 2nd ed (London: Macmillan, 1892), pp. 33–35, 'The Divine Names in the Epistle'

figure of the gospel story, the historical figure whose work 'yesterday' was God's decisive redemptive act 'in these last days' (1.2). Little is said in detail of his life, though more is said than is sometimes supposed. He became man (2.5–18), 'like his brethren in every respect' except sin (2.17; 4.15). This implies pre-existence and incarnation and entrance upon a form of life 'lower than the angels' (2.9). He had to 'share in flesh and blood' (2.14) to become able to help men, but the 'How' of the incarnation is not discussed. It was necessary for him to have 'suffered and been tempted' to be 'able to help those who are tempted' (2.18). He had to withstand temptation; he can help men only because he 'in every respect has been tempted as we are, yet without sinning' (4.15).

Hebrews is the one New Testament writing outside the Synoptic Gospels which frankly and clearly states that Jesus was tempted. But it differs from the Synoptics as to the time and function of the temptation. In the Synoptics Jesus is tempted after his baptism and before the opening of his public ministry (Mark 1.9–15); the Gethsemane struggle (Mark 14.32–42) is not clearly treated as his climactic temptation. In Heb. 5.7–9, however, it is the Gethsemane struggle that seems chiefly and clearly in mind, though this is not explicitly stated. In that crucial test he 'learned obedience through what he suffered' and by his faithfulness under temptation he was 'made perfect' and so was competent to act decisively to save and purify men. This salvation 'was declared at first by the Lord' Jesus (2.3); the author of Hebrews knows that Jesus had a teaching ministry. But this was not the author's real interest; it was the human Gethsemane struggle wherein Jesus learned to be fully obedient under the test of suffering which was of crucial importance. The maturity of victory over temptation was the necessary qualification for his real ministry.[13]

So in a sense Jesus' earthly life and ministry and even his acceptance of death, when he 'suffered outside the gate' of Jerusalem (13.12), were only necessary—but really necessary—preliminaries for his effective high priestly ministry. The author of Hebrews, as we shall understand better when we come to our next section on Jesus' sacrifice, both magnifies and minimizes Jesus' earthly life and temptation and physical death.

It is a good clue to the centre of interest of this author that in all

---

[13] See R. V. G. Tasker, *The Gospel in the Epistle to the Hebrews* (London: Tyndale Press, 1950), Ch. II, 'The Fulfilment', p. 33.

his discussion of the death of Jesus he never explicitly refers to Jesus' resurrection. His thought hurries on past the earthly triumph over physical death, which is only implied in 13.20, to the heavenly ministry and triumph. For the statement that 'God ... brought again from the dead our Lord Jesus' means something more than the rising of Jesus to renewed life on this earth; it includes and mainly concerns the bringing of Jesus into the heavenly setting where his real priestly ministry is carried out.

(ii) *Christ*. The title Christ, as has been noted, is used without any clear reference to the traditional messianic role and functions. The author knows that Jesus 'was descended from Judah' (7.14), and so in his discussion he might have made use of the expectation of a Davidic Messiah. But he makes nothing of this Davidic connection and his use of the title Christ has much the same sweep as have the references to Jesus.

Pre-existence is assumed; Christ was 'faithful over God's house' (3.6). He did not usurp the role of high priest, but 'was appointed' to it by God (5.5). He carried out a redemptive ministry as high priest (9.11–14); this involved his being 'offered once to bear the sins of many' (9.28). He will complete his work; he 'will appear a second time ... to save those who are eagerly waiting for him' (9.28). The title Christ has become little if anything more than another proper name referring to Jesus.

(iii) *Jesus Christ*. This loss of the original meaning of the word Christ, the completed development from a title indicating messianic role to a proper name, is confirmed by the use of the designation Jesus Christ in 10.10; 13.8, 21. These two words constitute a compound proper name. They refer quite clearly in 10.10 to the death of the historical person Jesus Christ and to his sacrificial offering to deal decisively with human sin; we read there of the 'offering of the body of Jesus Christ once for all'. Since, as the next chapter on 'A Sacrifice For Sin' will show, this offering occurs in the heavenly sanctuary, there is no conflict but rather a deep interrelation between this 'offering of the body of Jesus Christ' and the result that the exalted 'Jesus Christ is the same yesterday and today and for ever' (13.8).

The formal benediction in 13.20–21 uses 'Jesus Christ' as a proper name synonymous with 'our Lord Jesus'. The author prays that 'through Jesus Christ', now 'brought again from the dead', God may 'equip you [the Christians addressed] with everything good that you may do his will, working in you that which is pleasing in his sight' (13.20–21). 'Through Jesus Christ' refers not only to the purification of sinners from past sins through the work of Jesus Christ, but also to God's continuing active ministry through him for the enrichment and healthy development of Christians in a life of faithful obedience to the divine will. The picture emerges of a continuing ministry of the exalted Christ.

(iv) *The Son.* Jesus is not called 'the Son' in chapter 13, but the title is used eleven times of him in seven of the preceding twelve chapters. The main question is whether what is said of the Son is essentially present in other terms used in chapter 13.

Hebrews knows of no time when the Son did not exist or will not exist. Through him God 'created the world', through all time he upholds 'the universe by his word of power', and he it is whom God 'appointed the heir of all things'; he is divine, for 'he reflects the glory of God and bears the very stamp of his nature' (1.2–3). He is called 'God' in 1.8–9 and divine 'Lord' in 1.10. Over God's world, which the Son created (1.2), over 'God's house', which especially means God's people Israel to which Moses was 'a servant', Christ was faithful 'as a son' (3.6).

The reference to God's Son as 'begotten', in a quotation from Ps. 2.7 (1.5; 5.5), does not refer to bringing the Son into being before the creation of the world, nor is it probable that the birth into human life is meant; the reference seems rather to his exaltation and installation (after his earthly death) on the 'throne' of his 'kingdom' (1.8). He has 'passed through the heavens' (4.14) and 'sat down at the right hand of the Majesty on high' (1.3). 'Although he was a Son, he learned obedience through what he suffered' at the climax of his earthly career, and only after he was matured and 'made perfect' by suffering did he become by his sacrifice 'the source of eternal salvation to all who obey him' (5.8–9). Then he was truly 'a Son who has been made perfect for ever' (7.28), and as the Melchizedek comparison indicates, 'he continues a priest for ever' (7.3).

This description of the career and work of Jesus as the Son is essentially the portrait which Hebrews gives of 'Jesus' the 'Christ'. It is in agreement with what 13.8, 12, 20–21 reflect of the author's viewpoint, though chapter 13 does not use the title Son. It is reasonable to say that chapter 13 is in harmony with what the

earlier chapters say about 'a great high priest who has passed
through the heavens, Jesus, the Son of God' (4.14).

(v) *High Priest*.[14] The title of Jesus that is most prominent in
Hebrews is 'high priest'. The author may refer to priests, but his
interest is not in the priestly group but in the high priest as seen
in the Levitical law, and he thinks of that high priest even when
he seems to speak only of an ordinary 'priest'. Moreover, he is
interested only in the ministry of the high priest on the Day of
Atonement (9.7). He does speak of the daily offerings of the
Levitical priest (10.11), but his real concern is with the annual Day
of Atonement ceremony; the real comparison he makes is between the high priest's yearly offering on the Day of Atonement
and the once for all offering by Christ (10.12).

It is important to note the qualifications which Jesus has as the
one true high priest. By coming into human life he became one
of his people, 'like his brethren in every respect', and so could
'become a merciful and faithful high priest in the service of God,
to make expiation for the sins of the people' (2.17-18). He could
'sympathize with our weaknesses', for he 'has been tempted as we
are' (4.15). Yet he met temptation 'without sinning' (4.15), and so
as 'holy, blameless, unstained' he had no need to offer sacrifices for
his own sins, but was qualified to proceed to the offering of a
sacrifice for the sins of his people (7.26-28).

He did not demand or seize the high priestly role; he was
appointed by God (5.5). 'In the days of his flesh' he 'learned obedience through what he suffered' and so achieved the mature per-
fection which qualified him to act as the one true and effective high
priest (5.7-9). He is now 'high priest for ever' (6.20) and is seated
'at the right hand' of God (8.1), which indicates both his glory and
his authority.

With all of these qualifications, Christ the high priest 'offered
for all time a single sacrifice for sins' and then 'sat down at the

[14] A well known study of the priesthood of Jesus is that of Alexander
Nairne, *The Epistle of Priesthood* (Edinburgh: T. and T. Clark, 1913). See
especially chapters 5 and 6 of his book. From a basis in more recent studies
Oscar Cullmann, in *The Christology of the New Testament*, tr. Shirley C. Guthrie
and Charles A. M. Hall (London: SCM Press, and Philadelphia: Westminster
Press, 1959), p. 85, agrees with Ernst Käsemann (see note 18 below) that
before Hebrews was written there existed a Melchizedek speculation 'which
is of partly Jewish, partly Christian-Gnostic origin'. However, as we have
said, the author of Hebrews does not use the figure of Melchizedek in defining
the priestly role and work of Jesus.

right hand of God' to wait for the complete subjection of his enemies (10.12–13) and finally to 'appear' on earth 'a second time' to 'save those who are eagerly waiting for him' (9.28).

In using this title the author passes freely from 'high priest' to the name Jesus or to some other title (3.1; 4.14; 5.10; 6.20; 7.28; 8.6; 9.11, 27; 10.12). The obvious inference is that these titles largely overlap; each is used to bring out one aspect of who Jesus was and what he did, and all are used to refer to Jesus, whose historical appearance and action are the focal concern of the author and whose person and work can only be properly understood and appreciated by the use of a number of titles, of which he considers 'high priest' to be the most significant and instructive.

Chapter 13 does not use the title 'high priest' to refer to Jesus. But as will become clearer in the next chapter on 'A Sacrifice For Sin', Jesus the high priest is viewed in Hebrews as both sacrificing priest and sacrificial victim. Now we read in 13.12 that 'Jesus ... suffered outside the gate' of Jerusalem, just as in the Levitical ceremony on the Day of Atonement the bodies of the animals whose blood is brought into the sanctuary by the high priest are burned outside the camp. So we are justified in concluding that the author has in mind here as in the earlier chapters the total role of Jesus as the great high priest.

(vi) *Lord.* The title Lord is used of Jesus as well as of God. In 2.3 the author refers to the fact that 'such a great salvation ... was declared at first by the Lord'. This seems to refer, at least in part, to the preaching of Jesus, though Moffatt sees here a reference 'not specifically to his teaching, but to his personality and career'.[15] This passage is in any case a clear reference to the historical Jesus, concerning whom the author knows that 'our Lord was descended from Judah' (7.14).

But the use of 'Lord' for Jesus has a wider reference than to designate the historical Jesus. The pre-existence and the divine role of the Lord (Jesus) as creator of 'the earth' and 'the heavens' is attested in 1.10–12, a passage which affirms that he will continue everlastingly to hold this title. It thus is not surprising that 13.20 speaks of the exalted and glorified Jesus as 'our Lord Jesus'; he is the living and present Lord of his people.

[15] James Moffatt, *The Epistle to the Hebrews* (International Critical Commentary; Edinburgh: T. and T. Clark, and New York: Charles Scribner's Sons, 1924), p. 19.

It may even be suggested that 'the Lord' in the thrice used phrase 'says the Lord' in 8.8, 9, 10 is a reference to Jesus Christ as the high priest. To us this may seem unnatural, for we know that 8.8–12 quotes Jer. 31.31–34, and 'lord' in these verses represents a Greek word (κύριος) behind which lies 'Yahweh' in the Hebrew. But we must remember from 1.8–12 that the author's method of using Scripture permitted him to use both 'God' in Ps. 45.7 and 'Lord' in the Septuagint of Ps. 102.26 (EVV 102.25) as a reference to the divine Son. Now in 8.6 the author speaks of Christ as the high priest (the subject 'Christ' supplied by the RSV in 8.6 is not in the Greek; this interpretation is correct, however, for the context speaks of Christ as the high priest). He is said to mediate a better covenant. So when without a new subject 8.8 goes on to quote words of Scripture as the utterance of the maker of the 'new covenant', and those words are said three times to be the utterance of 'the Lord', the tentative suggestion may be made that by 'the Lord' the author here means the high priest, Jesus.[16]

In any case, 13.20 shows that chapter 13 is in essential agreement with chapters 1–12 in using 'the Lord' as a title of Jesus the great high priest.

(vii) *Shepherd*. Only in 13.20 does Hebrews use this title of Jesus (cf. Matt. 18.12–14; Luke 15.4–7; John 10.1–18; I Peter 2.25; 5.4; Rev. 7.17). But a high priest who is merciful (2.17), who can and does 'sympathize with our weaknesses' (4.15), and whose concern for his people is such that 'he always lives to make intercession for them' (7.25), is aptly described in 13.20 as 'the great shepherd of the sheep'.

(viii) *Apostle*. The author makes no use of the term 'apostle' to designate companions of Jesus or leaders of the Church. But in one passage (3.1) he speaks of Jesus as 'the apostle and high priest of our confession'. The word apostle (ἀπόστολος) means one sent on a mission. The Church, implied in the word 'our', is to give grateful and reverent attention and thought to Jesus, who as apostle was sent by God to carry out his ministry as high priest.

---

[16] This cannot be proved. But we may be too slow to refer to Jesus Old Testament passages that speak of Yahweh and are rendered κύριος in the Septuagint. See the bold claims of A. T. Hanson in his book, *Jesus Christ in the Old Testament* (London: SPCK, 1965). On the term Lord see *Bible Key Words* 2 (London: A. and C. Black, and New York: Harper and Brothers, 1958). It gives an English translation of the article on κύριος in *TWNT*, written by Werner Foerster and Gottfried Quell.

As God's emissary he was authorized to speak and act for the salvation of his people and to be the Lord of their fellowship and life and their future.

The title apostle is a passing reference in one passage in chapters 1–12, so there is no reason to expect it in chapter 13, whose content is not concentrated on Christology and salvation but mainly on varied exhortations and personal messages. The title suggests nothing out of harmony with the basic attitude of chapter 13.

(ix) *God*. Only in 1.8–9 do we find this striking designation for Jesus the Son.[17] In more than one title, however, the author witnesses that Jesus the Christ, the Son, the High Priest, the Lord, exercised divine functions, both in creating and upholding the world and in redeeming and blessing his people (cf. e.g. 1.2–3 and I Cor. 8.6). Not long after Hebrews was written, John 1.1 can say in simple words and with bold audacity that 'the Word was God'. This was essentially what Hebrews had already confessed. It was because this was the faith of the author that he could ascribe to Jesus Christ 'glory for ever and ever' (13.21).

It is clear that when we examine the ways in which Hebrews speaks of Jesus Christ, an essential agreement emerges between the references in chapters 1–12 and those in chapter 13.

4. 'A SACRIFICE FOR SIN'

These words are used in 13.11 of the blood which in the Levitical system 'is brought into the sanctuary by the high priest as a sacrifice for sin'. 13.12 indicates that the words may be applied to Jesus: 'So Jesus also suffered outside the gate in order to sanctify the people through his own blood.' Indeed, chapters 7–10 in particular centre upon the fact that Jesus as the 'great high priest' (4.14) offered the once-for-all and only effective sacrifice for sin. This is the heart of the argument of Hebrews.

The reference of course is to the historical event of the death of Jesus and to its full setting and effect. Jesus was 'crowned with glory and honour because of the suffering of death, so that by the grace of God he might taste death for every one' (2.9). The purpose of his death is clearly stated; it was 'purification for sins'

---

[17] In 1.8 the Son is clearly called God. In 1.9 this is not so clear, but it seems probable (as in the NEB).

(1.3). 'He has appeared once for all at the end of the age to put away sin by the sacrifice of himself' (9.26).

Only once is the aim to defeat the devil stated; Jesus shared the 'flesh and blood' nature and life 'that through death he might destroy him who has the power of death, that is, the devil, and deliver all those who through fear of death were subject to lifelong bondage' (2.14–15). The main attention is given to his sacrifice for sin. It is assumed that all men have sinned and cannot themselves deal with sin and its guilt and power. They need a remedy which only divine resources can provide. It is assumed that only an effective sacrifice in which blood is shed and offered can deal effectively with this sin.

The author of Hebrews does not look to the Old Testament Law and its literal provisions to give the solution. (Note that when he speaks of the Law he does not mean the Pentateuch as a body of legal prescriptions; he is far removed from this Pauline viewpoint; he thinks essentially of the Levitical prescriptions and their possible efficacy in dealing with sin.) That Law, 'because of its weakness and uselessness . . . made nothing perfect' (7.18–19).

The main reason was not that the priests who officiated under that law were sinful and mortal human beings, though this was a real defect in the Levitical system (7.23, 27), but that its system of animal sacrifice can never deal effectively with human wrongdoing: 'It is impossible that the blood of bulls and goats should take away sins' (10.4). The Levitical 'gifts and sacrifices . . . cannot perfect the conscience of the worshipper, but deal only with food and drink and various ablutions, regulations for the body imposed until the time of reformation' (9.9–10). To the author the Levitical system prefigures the work of Christ, but it was not effective, and now that Christ has dealt decisively with sin that ancient system is superseded and no longer in force.

It is clear that in Hebrews Jesus is the effective high priest qualified to make the effective offering. But what is the effective offering? The answer is clear. Jesus is both the high priest who presents the offering and the offering that he presents.

This assigning of a double role to Jesus may seem a glaring blunder, but it is perhaps the deepest spiritual insight which Hebrews has to offer. The only complete and effective offering which a person can make is the offering of oneself. The true offering is not the giving of things but the giving of oneself in willing obedience: 'I have come to do thy will, O God' (10.7, quoting Psalm 40.7–8). 'He offered up himself' (7.27); it was a once-for-all fully effective sacrifice; he 'offered for all time a single sacrifice for sins' (10.12). No other priest will ever be needed; no other sacrifice for sin can ever be made. This sacrifice is adequate, effective, complete, once for all.

But where does Jesus the great high priest make this sacrifice? Where does he present this offering? A correct understanding of the message of Hebrews depends on finding the right answer to this question. There are many Christians who would say that Jesus offered himself on the cross on Calvary. This answer contains an element of truth. Jesus died a real death on earth, and Christian tradition knew from the first that this key event of the gospel story took place just outside the city of Jerusalem. But this does not yet grasp and state the thinking of the author of Hebrews.

He was not concerned seriously with earthly geography. Even the relation of the crucifixion to Jerusalem and specifically to a spot 'outside the gate' (13.12) is a minor point in his total view. Above all, he has no concern to parallel what happened to Jesus with what went on in the Temple at Jerusalem. As we have already pointed out, he thinks in the framework of the Levitical provisions in the Pentateuch. In the wilderness setting of the journeying people of Israel,[18] he thinks of the portable Tent as the setting of the high priest's ministry on the Day of Atonement. He had in mind especially Leviticus 16.

He does not think of the sanctuary in which Jesus offered himself as a copy of the Tent in which Aaron was to minister. His idea is just the reverse. The original Tent, the 'true tent' (8.2), was and is the one in heaven. Of this 'true tent', this 'heavenly sanctuary', the one that Moses made was but 'a copy and shadow' (8.5; 9.23–24). The author understands Ex. 25.40 to speak of such a heavenly sanctuary, shown to Moses on the mountain and used by him as the original from which he made an earthly copy in portable form for use by the journeying people of God.[19]

[18] Ernst Käsemann, in *Das wandernde Gottesvolk*, 2nd ed. (Göttingen: Vandenhoeck and Ruprecht, 1957), has demonstrated the basic role which this theme of the journeying people of God plays in the thought of Hebrews.

[19] Two instructive studies of the heavenly sanctuary are Franz Joseph Schierse, *Verheissung und Heilsvollendung* (München: Karl Zink Verlag, 1955), Part I, and Aelred Cody, *Heavenly Sanctuary and Liturgy in the Epistle to the Hebrews* (St Meinrad, Indiana: Grail Publications, 1960).

In this wilderness sanctuary the author's main interest is directed to the portable Tent. It has two compartments. The 'outer' Tent or Holy Place was behind a curtain which hung at the entrance to set it apart; it was served by the priests, who could 'go continually into' it (9.6).

Behind the 'second' curtain stood 'the Holy of Holies' (9.3–5). The author of Hebrews seems to locate the altar of incense in this Holy of Holies, although in fact the Pentateuchal regulations placed it in the Holy Place though near to the 'second curtain' and the Holy of Holies (Ex. 30.6).[20] But he had little interest in the Holy Place and its furnishings. His attention was directed to the Holy of Holies, into which only the high priest could enter, and he only on the Day of Atonement each year. On that day he entered the Holy of Holies twice, the first time with blood of a bullock as the sin offering for himself, and the second time with blood of a goat as the sin offering for the people (Lev. 16).

While this earthly Tent was in general 'a copy and shadow' of the true sanctuary in heaven, it differed in certain important respects:

(i) The Levitical Tent was purified and consecrated by 'the blood of calves and goats' (9.19), but the heavenly sanctuary 'with better sacrifices' (9.23),[21] which quite clearly refers to the blood of Jesus (9.11–14).

(ii) The earthly wilderness Tent was served by a continual succession of mortal priests, while Jesus the great high priest 'brought again from the dead' (13.20), 'holds his priesthood permanently, because he continues for ever' (7.24).

(iii) The Levitical high priests made their sin offerings yearly on the Day of Atonement, but Jesus 'entered once for all into the Holy Place' (which here refers to the heavenly sanctuary and in particular to the inner sanctuary, the Holy of Holies). By that one effective sacrifice and offering he made an effective and complete 'purification for sins' (9.11–12; 1.3).

(iv) The Levitical high priest had to enter the Holy of Holies twice on each Day of Atonement, the first time with blood to car-

[20] On the location of the altar of incense see Bruce, *op. cit.*, pp. 184–7.

[21] The idea that the heavenly sanctuary needed to be purified may seem almost blasphemous to some Christians in our day. But that is the plain meaning of 9.23. The language is figurative but it is not idle talk. The sanctuary had to be purified, consecrated, and set apart for the high priestly ministry.

for his own sins, and only then with blood to offer 'for the errors of the people' (9.7). Since Jesus was sinless, made perfect by withstanding temptation and suffering, he had no need to make an offering for himself. He needed only to enter the Holy of Holies once to offer his own blood as the once-for-all sacrifice for men's sins.

In fact, the author of Hebrews seems at the end to concentrate all his interest on the Holy of Holies and he practically comes to think of heaven as the Holy of Holies. Heaven, like the Holy of Holies, is the place where God dwells or is encountered, where men 'draw near to God through him' (7.25). 9.24 comes close to an explicit identification of the heavenly 'sanctuary' with 'heaven itself'. It clearly implies such an identification. And in 10.19–20 the thought of the sanctuary as a place into which only the high priest enters opens up into the view that Christ's people can 'enter the sanctuary by the blood of Jesus, by the new and living way which he opened for us through the curtain'. Thus a new, free, and full access to God is opened up by the high-priestly work of Christ.

The author's conception of the heavenly sanctuary is remarkable. It existed when Moses was instructed to make the Tent as a copy of it (8.5). But there is no idea of its use until 'in these last days' (1.2). It was purified when entered by Jesus with his own blood at the time of his sacrifice for sins (9.23–24). Since that time when Jesus made his once-for-all sacrifice for sin, it has not been used nor will it ever be used again as a place of sacrifice. If any further ministry of the high priest in the heavenly sanctuary is in mind, it is Jesus' intercession for his people, for 'he always lives to make intercession for them' (7.25). In all the ages the true sanctuary was used for only one sacrificial offering for sin, but that, the author holds, was adequate to meet the need of sinners.

Chapter 13 contains few hints of this complex conception of the heavenly sanctuary and the one sacrifice for sin. But the discussion of the next section on 'We Have an Altar' will show that the final chapter of Hebrews assumes the same priestly and sacrificial setting that we find in the earlier chapters. The references to 'an altar' and to the Tent in 13.10 clearly imply that setting. The contrast between the sacrificial use of animal blood and Jesus' 'own blood', and the mention of the fact that the bodies of the animals slain as a sin offering were 'burned outside the camp', use the Levitical regulations to assert the superior sacrifice of Jesus (13.11–13). It is only by reference to chapters 1–12 that we can understand fully the author's allusions to sacrifice in chapter 13, but the brief data in the latter chapter fit well with what the earlier chapters say concerning Jesus' sacrifice for sin.

5. 'WE HAVE AN ALTAR'

In discussing the Day of Atonement ministry of the Levitical high priest, the author of Hebrews focused attention on the Tent and particularly on its two compartments, the Holy Place and the Holy of Holies. He showed no interest in the altar, which was an integral part of the Levitical worship setting; only 7.13 shows that he was aware that this worship setting included an altar. Now, however, in 13.10, comes a brief and quite puzzling reference: 'We have an altar from which those who serve the tent have no right to eat.'

It is clear from the use of the word 'we' that this altar is a Christian altar. Whatever it means, it refers to an instrument of worship by Christian believers. Since the wilderness Tent with its altar of burnt offering (Ex. 27.1–8) was to the author of Hebrews only 'a copy and shadow of the heavenly sanctuary' (8.5), and the only relevant sanctuary for the Christian is that heavenly one, we must conclude that the altar which the Christians have must be a part of that total heavenly sanctuary.

Thus the Christian altar cannot be the one in the temple court at Jerusalem. The author never shows any interest in the Jerusalem temple. It is true that 13.11–12 includes a passing allusion to the Jerusalem of Jesus' day, for the fact that 'Jesus . . . suffered outside the gate' clearly has in mind Jesus' death just outside the Jerusalem walls. But the interweaving of Septuagint wording into these two verses, and especially the reference in 13.11 to Jesus suffering 'outside the *camp*', shows that the author's real interest is in the wilderness Tent described in the Pentateuch, and in chapters 7–10 it is on this Tent that he concentrates all his interest.

Nor can the Christian altar be the one which Israel was said to have made and used in the wilderness. It belonged to the 'copy and shadow' order of things (8.5) and not to the heavenly sanctuary where the Christian altar must be sought.

Neither would it be satisfactory to identify the Christian altar with the earthly cross. There would be some justification for doing

this, for the gospel story, in Hebrews as elsewhere, blends historical earthly features with events and setting in the heavenly scene.
But the message of Hebrews is that the once-for-all offering which
Jesus made was an offering made by blood in the heavenly
sanctuary. (This image, of course, comes from the Day of Atonement ritual of Leviticus 16.) It would not fit the author's viewpoint to say that the Christian altar is on earth while the true
sanctuary is in heaven. The true sanctuary, including the true
altar, is the heavenly sanctuary.

For similar reasons it will not do to identify the Christian altar
with the table of the Church's Lord's Supper. An altar is a place
of sacrifice. The sacrifice in Hebrews is Christ the high priest's
once-for-all offering of himself. To connect with the Lord's
Supper the idea of the repeated sacrifice of Christ would be to
disregard and falsify the author's basic conception of the great
high priest and his once-for-all sacrifice in the heavenly sanctuary,
where we must conclude the Christian altar is thought to be
located.[22]

A decision as to the meaning of 13.10 depends on the meaning
of 'the tent' in this verse and the relation of this verse to its context. It is clear that the 'altar' here refers to the Christian altar in
the heavenly sanctuary. Does 'the tent' refer to the wilderness
Tent described in the Pentateuch or does it also refer to that
heavenly worship setting?

If it refers to the wilderness Tent, then 'those who serve the
tent' are Israelites, and more specifically the Levitical priests,
especially the Levitical high priests, whose duties are set down
in the Pentateuch. In that case the verse means that we Christians
have an altar from which the Levitical priests, and presumably
also the priests of the later Jewish worship, have no right to eat.
They cannot officiate in the Levitical sacrifices and also eat from the
Christian altar.

On this view one could think of Acts 6.7: 'A great many of the
priests were obedient to the faith', and conjecture that some of the
priests who had believed in Jesus were continuing in their priestly
duties (this would date Hebrews before the fall of Jerusalem) and

---

[22] Johannes Behm, in the article on θυσιαστήριον in *TWNT* III (1938),
pp. 182–3, says that the reference is neither to the cross nor to the Lord's
table; there is only a general idea that there are no sacrificial meals in the
New Testament sacrificial system.

at the same time were taking part in the meals and Lord's Supper of the Church. The author of Hebrews would be asserting that this is a compromising double loyalty which is not right.

It is conceivable that such a situation arose and was tolerated by some Christians but odious to the author of Hebrews. If so, however, we could reasonably have expected clearer evidence than we have here. It therefore seems probable that in 13.10 the author is speaking of the heavenly sanctuary not only in his reference to the altar but also in his words about the Tent. A careful study of the context will tend to confirm this conclusion.

At first sight it may seem that 13.7–16 is made up of an unconnected series of unrelated statements and exhortations. The passage does have a wide-ranging character, but on close examination the successive statements and exhortation are seen to be rather clearly related. We here follow these thought links far enough to grasp the context in which 13.10 must be understood.

After speaking of the faithfulness of God in caring for his people (13.5b–6), the author recalls the faithfulness of the now deceased leaders of the Christians addressed, and he urges the latter to imitate the faith (which includes faithfulness) of those leaders. Such stable loyalty will find its best pattern in Jesus Christ; his loyalty under testing and his obedience even in suffering offer to Christians the supreme example of such faithful living. His steadfast integrity and perfected character give his followers an exemplar who is dependably 'the same yesterday and today and for ever' (13.8).

Therefore they should not 'be led away by diverse and strange teachings', but should manifest a similar stable obedience to God (13.9). This false teaching which the author opposes is not a single consistent doctrine but is rather 'diverse' and so quite varied and volatile. But it is implied that in its various forms it is 'strange' in comparison with the basic gospel message, and it concerns rules and practices about 'foods', rules and practices which, the author is certain, 'have not benefited their adherents'.

Just what these food rules were is not certain. There are at least four possible views on this question.

(i) The reference just possibly could be to Jewish laws about clean and unclean foods. But the reference in that case could not be simply to the Pentateuchal food laws or merely to the oral traditions of Pharisaic Judaism concerning such laws. For those laws and traditions were on the whole a consistent and known system rather than 'diverse and strange'. If Jewish food laws are in mind, they must be regulations of some syncretistic and perhaps ascetic Jewish group or sect. If these food laws are variations and unusual applications of the Levitical food laws, then 'those who serve the tent' in 13.10 would seem to refer to Jewish priests, and it is doubtful whether such priests would be involved in varied and changeable application of such laws. The champions of such 'diverse and strange teachings' about foods are not likely to be found among the functioning or legally qualified Jewish priests of the author's day.

(ii) A second possible explanation is that some ascetic sect was developing and promoting special, varied, and variable practices about foods. Such an ascetic sect could have been quite variable both in its membership and in its particular food regulations. Indeed, the situation could have been an ascetic and individualistic tendency, developed in various directions by various leaders and showing a freely variable range of dietary practices; it would not have been a unified cohesive sect with a regulated list of food rules. A loosely organized sect of this kind could conceivably have been a fringe sect within Hellenistic Judaism,[23] where the author of Hebrews could have known it, or it could have existed within the Gentile world if the author was addressing a largely Gentile group of Christians. The essential thing in the type of persons described is that they expected their spiritual lot to depend upon or at least be seriously affected by their observance of their food laws. The author is Pauline on this issue, for he denies that such food rules have any spiritual effectiveness; it is not 'foods' but divine 'grace' that will strengthen the heart and save and bless the believer (13.9).

(iii) A third possibility is that in 13.9 the author is opposing mystery cult practices in which the adherents believed that by the devouring of special foods they were literally eating the god and so becoming partakers of life and immortality. Such practices would of course have been Gentile in origin, but in that syncretistic day it is not inconceivable that such tendencies found partial acceptance in Jewish and Christian circles which wanted to be 'progressive' and *en rapport* with the secular world. Those were days in which a proto-Gnostic claim to 'knowledge' and the

---

[23] Such a group could hardly have been the Qumran sect, which was a strongly organized and sternly disciplined sect.

adoption of syncretistic practices were at work,[24] and a Christian teacher could have had sound reason for sober warnings. If the beginnings of such mystery cult practices were in the author's mind, he was thinking of abuses connected with the common meals of the Christians, including the memorial celebration of the Lord's Supper. The lack of any real contemporary evidence that the mystery cults had definite influence on Christian fellowship and worship in the first century, or that definitely crystallized Gnosticism was actively threatening the Church before the second century, makes one hesitate to find the background of 13.9 in the mystery cult conception of eating the god at special cult assemblies. If the author of Hebrews had known of such a practice in the Christian group addressed, he could have been expected to react against it with a horror of which 13.9 reveals no trace.

(iv) A fourth possible view is that in 13.9 the author is definitely thinking about an observance of the Lord's Supper in which, according to some Christians here in mind, the blessing and benefit depended on careful observance of what to the author were 'diverse and strange' and actually harmful teachings about the special efficacy of observing certain (here unstated) food rules. Such practices, the author would then imply, were not beneficial but were actually damaging, since they tended to look to 'foods' rather than to divine 'grace' for spiritual benefit from the Supper.

A combination of two or more of these four explanations is possible. As Colossians 2.16–23 makes clear, such 'philosophies', using Jewish food and other rules, adopting syncretistic practices, reflecting incipient stages of Gnosticism and mystery cults, and bringing practices of such kinds into the common memorial meal of the congregation, were beginning to appear.[25] It is impossible to identify clearly and in detail just what was developing in the situation which the author of Hebrews and the Christians he addressed were facing. It seems clear, however, that we should

[24] The presence of syncretistic tendencies in the first-century Near East is not to be denied. It is highly doubtful, however, whether before Christianity appeared this development had gone so far as to crystallize into the distinctively dualistic system and Gnostic redeemer myth for which the name Gnosticism should be reserved. See Johannes Munck, 'The New Testament and Gnosticism', in *Current Issues in New Testament Interpretation*, edited by William Klassen and Graydon F. Snyder (New York: Harper and Row, and London: SCM Press, 1962), pp. 224–38.

[25] T. W. Manson, *op. cit.*, p. 254, points out the parallel between Colossians and Hebrews.

interpret 13.9 in a way consistent with what we find stated in
13.10–12. What do these verses say?

As we have already noted, the crucial question in 13.10 is
whether 'the tent' refers to the wilderness worship centre of the
journeying people of Israel or to the heavenly sanctuary of which
chapters 7–10 speak in detail. If it is the former, then Levitical
priests are in mind, and it is said that they cannot minister in this
now superseded sanctuary and also eat from the altar of the
heavenly sanctuary to which the author here refers. That 'copy
and shadow' altar was never effective; its sacrifices could not 'take
away sins' (10.4). Only by the sacrifice of Christ, who is the great
high priest and is also the offering he makes, is 'purification for
sins' effected (1.3). The Levitical priests cannot combine the old
ministry of the Tent with the sacrifice Jesus made, which effective
sacrifice for sin is symbolized by the 'altar' in 13.10.

There is a basic flaw in the view just stated. It assumes that the
author thought of the heavenly altar as a place from which
Christians repeatedly eat; it assumes that they eat the sacrifice
made on that heavenly altar. This view does not fit into the
author's view. Jesus in his view offered a once-for-all sacrifice; it
was the free offering of himself; the blood of that sacrifice was
presented in the heavenly sanctuary and it made 'purification for
sins'. No further sacrifice is possible or needed. No Christian
believer, whether Jewish or Gentile, can combine other sacrifices
with this once-for-all sacrifice; there is no room for repeated sacrifices on the altar, sacrifices of which the Christian can eat.

If we put aside the idea that the author thought of repeated
sacrifices made on an altar from which Christians eat—and that
idea must be put aside, for it was not possible in view of the
author's total view—then we must take the word 'tent' to mean
the heavenly sanctuary and the 'altar' to mean the heavenly altar
which in the typology of Hebrews refers to Christ's once-for-all
sacrifice of himself.

The background of the author's thought was the annual Day
of Atonement offering for sins, made by the Levitical high priest.
In the Levitical ritual, sacrifices were slain close by the altar of
burnt offering. This idea is in the background here. And here
appears the key to the interpretation of 13.9–12. The animal
victim of that special Day of Atonement offering was not eaten
by the priests or other worshippers. As 13.11 recalls, the bodies of

those animals were taken outside the camp of the journeying children of Israel and burned.

So the way is barred, the author is saying, against any idea that Jesus as the once-for-all offering for sin can be thought of as eaten at Christian meals. Whatever the meaning of the meal Christians eat together, it is not a renewed sacrifice of Christ; it is not a meal which by some mysterious and almost magical power strengthens the worshippers 'by foods' rather than purely 'by grace' (13.9).[26]

We today think under the influence of the words at the Last Supper: 'Take; this is my body' (Mark 14.22; cf. I Cor. 11.24). We recall the words about Jesus as the bread of life and we remember his direction in John 6.35, 56 to eat his flesh and drink his blood. Regardless of how these words are interpreted, we must be careful to grasp and protect the full meaning of Hebrews, whose concern is to state, emphasize, and protect the once-for-all aspect of the self-offering of Christ. We must not let the thought of repeated sacrifice creep into the picture Hebrews gives of the way of man's redemption. In this concern 13.9–12 is in full agreement with the once-for-all offering of which chapters 7–10 so clearly speak.

6. 'THE ETERNAL COVENANT'

Behind the Old Testament worship to which Hebrews refers lay the covenant which God made in the wilderness with his journeying people Israel. There had been other covenants made with earlier individuals, who were thought of as representative of their descendants, and there were covenants after Moses' day which were thought of as renewals of the Sinai covenant that was made with Moses officiating (Ex. 24.8). But the Sinai covenant was one of the two key covenants of the Old Testament. The other was the promised 'new covenant' for whose coming Israel still looked at the end of the Old Testament period (Jer. 31.31–34). Hebrews deals with these two key covenants.[27]

Both are regarded as covenants with God's people. Certain Old

[26] See Moffatt, *op. cit.*, pp. 233–5.
[27] See the article on διαθήκη by Johannes Behm in *TWNT* II (1935), pp. 106–37, especially pp. 133–5. In the English translation of this great work, translated and edited by G. W. Bromiley, the article by Behm is in Vol. II, pp. 104–34, and the New Testament use of the word is discussed on pp. 129–34.

Testament covenants God seems to make with individuals, as in the case of God's covenant with Abraham (Gen. 17.2), but in such covenants the individual represents his family and/or descendants. The typical biblical thought concerning God's covenants, especially concerning the Sinai wilderness covenant and the promised covenant of Jer. 31.31–34, carries this sense of the social solidarity of those who share the covenant relationship to God.

This sense of a covenant with God's people is carried forward into the New Testament (Matt. 26.28; Mark 14.24; Luke 22.20 if authentic; Luke 22.29, $\delta\iota\alpha\tau\ell\theta\epsilon\mu\alpha\iota$; I Cor. 11.25; Gal. 3.15–17; and most frequently in Hebrews, where the word occurs seventeen times). The fact that the Church necessarily took its rise by the conversion of individuals to the Christian confession must not obscure from us this sense of the solidarity of believers, who share the covenant relationship with God and participate in a common faith and life. The author of Hebrews cannot understand how Christians as God's covenant people can neglect regular common worship and mutual helpfulness (10.23–25; 13.1).

In view of the importance of the covenant relation for the author of Hebrews, we must attempt to understand clearly how he understands the term covenant and the covenant relation of Christians to God.

The basic fact is that God of his free will and on his own initiative makes the covenant (8.8–10: 'I will establish', 'I made', 'I will make'). He is the superior and initiating party in establishing this relationship. The fact that two human individuals can make a covenant in which each has equal status must not obscure the superiority and initiative of God in his dealings with Israel and later with the Church. This was not an unparalleled type of covenant relationship. Recent studies of ancient treaties stating the basis of relationship between the chief sovereign of a region and his vassal kinglets show how a relationship could be formally established in which the sovereign ruler is clearly dominant; the relationship is established by his free decision and on his terms, which the subordinate party to the agreement accepts. This throws light on covenant relationships.[28] In the biblical covenants that we are studying the free action and initiative of God in making

---

[28] See Herbert H. Huffman, 'The Treaty Background of Hebrew Yāda'', *Bulletin of the American Schools of Oriental Research* No. 181 (February 1966), pp. 31–37.

the covenant are unmistakable. God (or Christ speaking for God) speaks of it as essentially 'my covenant' (8.9).

The covenant pledges God to give his people the promised privileges and benefits on the condition that his people fulfil the obligation of worship, obedience, and service to their God. It is of God's grace that they can enter into the covenant and receive its benefits, but they assume obligations and they agree to fulfil them as the condition for the continuance of the covenant relationship. In the case of the Sinai covenant, it is after Moses has read to the people 'the book of the covenant' and they have promised obedience to its requirements that Moses formally establishes the covenant of God with Israel (Ex. 24.7–8). It is the further miracle of God's grace in the biblical story that despite the failure of his people to keep their pledge of loyalty and obedience, God often renews the covenant and later promises and makes a better and truly effective new covenant.

In the New Testament accounts of the Last Supper it appears that it is upon the basis of Jesus' teaching and in particular upon the basis of his interpretation of his imminent death, a teaching and interpretation that the disciples implicitly accept, that they are asked to eat the bread and drink the wine, and in the early Church it is upon the basis of the Christians' acceptance of and obedience to the gospel of their redemption by the death of Christ that they enter and continue in the covenant realtionship. Like Old Testament Israel, the Christians by their sins break their promise and only God's continual grace keeps that relationship in force.

To the writer of Hebrews the shedding and offering of blood was indispensable for the establishing of the covenant and the meeting of men's spiritual need. In a way that is not convincing to modern thought, blood was thought to purify. 'Under the law almost everything is purified with blood, and without shedding of blood there is no remission of sins' (9.22). This holds true in the new covenant. Christ 'entered once for all into the Holy Place', that is, into the heavenly sanctuary, 'taking . . . his own blood' (9.11–12). The heavenly sanctuary was 'purified' and set apart when Jesus entered it with his own blood and 'made purification for sins' (9.23–24; 1.3).

The effect of the blood is not limited to these basic initial acts. The blood of animals can only sanctify 'for the purification of the flesh', but 'the blood of Christ' is able to 'purify your consciences from dead works to serve the living God' (9.13–14). 'The blood of the covenant' sanctifies; but for him who profanes it, spurns the Son of God, and outrages the Spirit of grace by sin, the extremest punishment waits (10.29).

The Greek word used for 'covenant' in Hebrews is διαθήκη. By general agreement among scholars this Greek word is translated 'covenant' wherever it occurs in Hebrews except in one passage, where the AV translates it 'testament' (9.15–20) and the RSV translates it 'will' (9.16–17).

The interpretation of the word as a 'will' by the RSV translators evidently was chosen because of the author's statement that the arrangement intended is one which goes into effect only when 'the death of the one who made it' can 'be established'. This does not fit the usual practice in making a covenant; as Ex. 24.1–8 shows, it is sufficient that the blood of an animal be used in making a valid covenant. And if God makes the covenant, as one might conclude on the basis of 8.8–10; 9.20; and 10.16,[29] one would be ready to add that God is the eternal God and will never die, so that if his death were necessary to put a covenant in force, it could never be established.

But this was not an ordinary covenant. The mediator who acted to establish it was not a sinful human being, like Moses, who acted in establishing the Sinai covenant. He was Jesus Christ the divine Son, whose will and action were one with the will and act of God himself. And the blood used in establishing this new covenant was not animal blood such as Moses used and called 'the blood of the covenant' (Ex. 24.8). It was the blood of Christ the perfected high priest, who was both ministering priest and sacrificial victim; he offered himself, his own blood (9.12). Because of his complete oneness in will and act with God his Father, what he does and what God does in making the covenant cannot be clearly distinguished; the testamentary arrangement which he makes and seals by his blood is the doing of God. So the author of Hebrews

---

[29] We pointed out earlier (in note 16) that in such passages as 8.8–10 and 10.16 the word 'Lord' just possibly could be taken to mean not God but 'our Lord Jesus' (13.20). Here again, in speaking of the διαθήκη, the roles of God and the Son are hard or perhaps impossible to keep clearly separate. The absolutely necessary thing in the author's mind is that in such an arrangement as a διαθήκη there must be shedding and use of blood in inaugurating the divinely given order. The death of Jesus and the presentation of his blood satisfied that requirement.

can affirm that this new covenant was a unique God-given covenant, which takes effect only when a death occurs and in connection with which the death of 'the one who made it' *can* 'be established' (9.16).

We need to keep our conception of the new covenant that Christ made elastic enough to allow for this unique situation. It is a 'testamentary disposition', as Moffatt calls it.[30] It requires the death of Christ who made it, a death that is thought of as connected with the shedding of blood, Christ's own blood. The fact that according to the gospel narratives of the passion Jesus' death by crucifixion was not due essentially to loss of blood does not affect the author's position. If he knew that loss of blood occurred in crucifixion, he had a basis and suggestion for his imagery. (The shedding of blood in John 19.34 *followed* death.) His essential point was that the new covenant was inaugurated not with the sacrifice of an animal but with the voluntary self-sacrifice of Jesus the great high priest who by his blood 'made purification for sins' (1.3).

The author makes rather frequent contrast between the Sinai covenant and the covenant made in Christ. The Sinai covenant was made with Israel, with Moses acting on divine instruction. It is called the first covenant (8.7, 13; 9.1, 15, 18), in view of the later one which is thus called 'a second' (8.7). That first one had the 'ark of the covenant' carried by the journeying people of God (9.4); it was the 'ark of the covenant' because it was believed to have contained 'a golden urn holding the manna, and Aaron's rod that budded, and the tables of the covenant' which Moses received on Mount Sinai (9.4). It was the covenant 'made with their fathers', that is, with the wilderness generation of Israel (8.9). From the viewpoint of the author of Hebrews it was the old covenant; it is contrasted with the new one of which the author speaks.

In such references the author shows a historical sense. He knows of the making of the covenant, its breaking by disobedient Israel, the promise of a new covenant, and the fulfilment of that promise in the work of Christ. Yet as far as we know his thinking he has a very limited historical sense. He works basically from the Old Testament and from the gospel which 'was declared at first by the

[30] James Moffatt, *op. cit.*, pp. 127-8. Behm in his article in *TWNT* (see note 27) says that apart from 9.16 f. the word can be translated *Verfügung*, but in 9.16 f. he translates it *Testament*.

Lord, and . . . attested to us by those who heard him' (2.3). It is only the broad contrast between the old and the new covenants, rather than detailed historical development, that interests him. He has no concern for general political and social processes. And he is interested in the history of Israel mainly as a background which makes clear God's plan to save men through Christ and establish the new covenant.

This second covenant (8.7) is no mere revision or improvement of the first. After those days of disobedience, and in fulfilment of God's purpose and promise (8.9–10), the Lord has established a covenant the adequate description of which requires the use of at least four adjectives:

(i) It is, as we have noted, the 'second' covenant as contrasted with the 'first', that is, with the Sinai covenant.

(ii) It is 'new', a radically new, decisive, effective, and once-for-all dealing with the sin and need of men (8.8, 13; 9.15; 12.24). With the passage of many centuries we have lost the sense of the thrilling newness of the gospel message. This author felt that newness vividly.

(iii) It is 'better' (7.22; 8.6); it is decidedly superior to the old covenant. In a sense, the use of this adjective 'better' is an understatement. The author was convinced that the sacrifice and blessing of the new covenant was unique and incomparably superior to what the old covenant could do. The continual sacrifices of animals could never perfect the worshippers; 'it is impossible that the blood of bulls and goats should take away sins' (10.4). The new sacrifice does what the old sacrifice could not accomplish.

But the author could not deny a value in the old covenant. Its sacrifices served to purify the flesh (9.13). It gave to the Church its Scripture. It pointed to the 'better' covenant which now had been established. It could not be disowned and discarded. But the 'new' was 'better', vastly and effectively better.

(iv) It is 'eternal'. We come back to chapter 13 prepared now to see that in the little it has to say about the covenant, it gives no reason to see anything discordant or different from what we have found in chapters 1–12. The covenant is 'eternal' (13.20); since it is a fully effective and solidly established covenant which does what it was intended to do, it will never need to be replaced, and so it will continue in force as God's eternal covenant. It is the covenant in force and valid since its recent establishment 'yesterday', it is effective 'today', and it will continue in force 'for ever' (13.8).

'Our Lord Jesus' is the ἔγγυος, the 'surety' (RSV) or 'guarantor' (NEB), of this covenant (7.22); he is its mediator who actually negotiates and inaugurates it. He guarantees its validity and effectiveness. He has brought men into this blessed relationship to God and since 'he always lives to make intercession for them' (7.25), they may rest confident that their future life and fellowship will be his concern and his working. This was the saving effect of 'the blood of the eternal covenant' and it will work out in the obedience to God's will which the life-purifying effect of that blood makes possible, This effect has come about and will come about 'through Jesus Christ, to whom' the grateful author ascribes 'glory for ever and ever' (13.21).

7. 'OUTSIDE THE CAMP'

In his argument that the sacrifice offered by the high priest on the Day of Atonement was one in which the body of the victim was not eaten, and that therefore the sacrifice for sins offered by Jesus as the 'great high priest' was one which permitted no eating of the sacrificial victim,[31] the author of Hebrews points out (13.11) that under the Levitical regulations the bodies of the animals sacrificed by the high priest on the Day of Atonement are taken 'outside the camp' and there burned (Lev. 16.27). In 13.12 the author carries this idea forward and applies it.

He notes that Jesus 'suffered outside the gate' to purify and 'sanctify the people' of God 'through his own blood'. Obviously he knew that Jesus was crucified outside the wall of Jerusalem, and he finds in this fact a real parallel to the procedure which Lev. 16.27 prescribes for the Day of Atonement. Just as the bodies of the sacrificial victims on the Day of Atonement were not eaten but were taken outside the camp and burned, so Jesus 'suffered outside the gate' and is not a part of the old sacrificial ceremonies observed at the Tent.

The author then proceeds to draw a conclusion from what he has said. The word 'therefore' in 13.13 indicates that he considers this conclusion to follow logically from what has preceded. He urges his readers to 'go forth to him [that is, to Jesus] outside the camp'. Actually, of course, the author thinks of Christ as having

[31] See our earlier discussion in ch. 3, section 5, 'We Have an Altar'.

entered the heavenly sanctuary, made purification for sins, and sat down at the right hand of God, which position of honour and authority does not keep him from carrying on a continual intercession for his people (7.25). He does not think of Jesus as permanently located just 'outside the gate' of the camp of the journeying people of God. But the exhortation to 'go forth to him outside the camp' urges the Christians addressed to break ties with whatever would prevent full loyalty to the Christ who offered himself as the once-for-all sacrifice for sins. Such a break would mean 'bearing abuse for him', but that is presented as the Christian's duty.

This going outside the camp is to the author symbolic of the break which Jesus made with the old order when he offered himself. Even if it was the fulfilment of the old Levitical system, it was the end of it as a legitimate way to seek forgiveness and fellowship with God. That Jesus suffered outside the gate and so outside the camp indicates that in a somewhat similar way his followers must 'go forth to him outside the camp'. They are no longer an integral part of the old order of worship and life. They live in a new order which offers and effects what the old order could only point to and promise. Those who believe in Jesus cannot continue to live in the old framework. They must 'go forth', and since that will bring them under criticism, they must willingly bear the reproach that will come to them as they live in this new situation.

This much is clear. The question that is difficult to answer is what meaning 13.13 gives to the word 'camp'. Does the author here use the word 'camp' to refer to the people of Israel in the author's day? In the wilderness situation the word certainly referred to Israel. The use in 13.11 of language recalling the Day of Atonement ceremony can be taken to imply that in 13.13 the author speaks to Christians who have a continuing participation in the worship and life of Judaism and summons them to move out of that setting in current Judaism and recognize that the worship and sacrificial practices of Judaism are a thing of the past. This would be the logical way to give to 'the camp' a meaning corresponding to its meaning in the journeying life of Israel in the wilderness.

Or is 'the camp' a figurative reference to the temporary situation of the Christian people of God in this world whose end is near at hand? Does the phrase thus refer to the created world in which all men now live but which has not long to last? Are the Christians being urged to 'sit loose' to the life of the world, to 'go forth' from it, and to live in separation from its pagan life? Is this a call to Christians to live an otherworldly life?

To put the alternatives more explicitly, there are at least three possible interpretations of the author's appeal to followers of Jesus to 'go forth to him outside the camp'.

As has just been suggested, this exhortation could be an appeal to them to separate sharply from the surrounding sinful world with its false worship and its worldly way of life. In that case it could be an appeal to Christians mostly of Gentile origin. It could be saying to them: You must break with all that is pagan and worldly and unworthy in the life of the world in which you are living 'in these last days'.

This view, which is widely held among scholars today,[32] is not without difficulty. It is not simply that the sentences in 13.11-15 have woven into them deliberate references to Septuagint language which call to mind the worship of the wilderness generations of Israel. It is even more the fact that the entire argument of Hebrews moves in the framework of the Levitical pattern of worship, especially the worship of the Day of Atonement. It continually contrasts that Israelite worship with the worship of God through Christ. None of the exhortations in this or the earlier chapters points to any pagan ways of worship and life from which the Christians addressed should 'go forth'.

It may be that the author was writing to Gentile Christians and appealing to them to break with Gentile patterns of worship and life and especially with pagan forms of fellowship which would compromise their Christian confession. But if that is so, the author has failed lamentably to give any statement of his concern that would suggest the pagan setting of the Christians to whom on this view he would be speaking. It would be a rather bookish and detached and unclear way of saying what he had to say.

A second possible interpretation of this appeal to 'go forth to him outside the camp' could be suggested by the recently gained knowledge of the Qumran sect.[33] If we include in our considera-

---

[32] E.g. James Moffatt, *op. cit.*, p. 235: 'a broad appeal for an unworldly religious fellowship'.

[33] The Qumran sect had broken with the priestly leadership at Jerusalem and withdrawn to the wilderness to protect the purity of its worship and life

ion the derogatory statement of 13.14 about the present city or
cities, it might be possible to take 13.13 as an appeal to leave
normal city life and withdraw into the wilderness. That the argument of Hebrews deals with the life of Israel in the wilderness days
would fit this conjecture. The author on this view might be saying
that the Christians addressed should separate from the city life and
public worship of Judaism. This would most readily suggest
separation from Jerusalem, and indicate that the letter was written
to a group of Christians in Jerusalem who were too ready to
remain an integral part of the Jewish worship there; in that case
13.13 would indicate a date for Hebrews prior to the Jewish war
with Rome and the resulting destruction of Jerusalem in AD 70.

But alternatively the summons to withdraw from the city life
of an urban Jewish settlement might be understood as an appeal
to separate from the Jewish synagogue and worship of some other
city where these Christians were living. It could conceivably refer
to Judaism in Rome, which was a city with a Jewish colony. But
this wilderness withdrawal interpretation is hardly convincing in
either form.

The third interpretation of the exhortation to 'go forth to him
outside the camp' would be to take it as an appeal to separate
entirely from Judaism. It could well be that there were Christians
who continued the ties with Judaism which the Church certainly
had in its earliest days. It is clear from the letters of Paul as well
as from the Acts that there was a general tendency in Gentile
churches to keep ties with Jewish Christians. Particularly where
Jewish Christians, possibly even including priests (cf. Acts 6.7),
were in a local church that was largely Gentile in membership,
there could have been a tendency of the entire group to continue
practices basic to Judaism. The result could have been an attempt
to share in both Jewish and Christian worship and practices, and
this could have led to at least an unconscious readiness to regard
these Jewish practices as essential to Christian life.

So whether the Christians addressed were Jewish in origin or
Gentiles who had become deeply attached to Jewish ways, the
situation could have arisen in which an exhortation was needed to
'go forth' to a clear Christian worship and a life definitely separate
from Judaism. This explanation would give to the word 'camp' its
natural meaning as a reference to the people of Israel.

This explanation gives an urgent reason for the contrasts which

Hebrews presents. It never faces the possibility that if, as seems to have happened (12.12–13), these Christians had become lax and discouraged, they might turn to Plato, Stoicism, Epicureanism, emperor worship, a mystery cult, or any other of the many world views and cults which flourished in the first-century Roman world. Such possible alternatives to the Christian confession are never mentioned or considered.

Every possible rival to Christ the author chooses from the Jewish background: the angels known from Scripture and active in giving the Law (2.2), Moses (3.2), Joshua (4.8), the high priest (4.14 and often), and the Day of Atonement sacrifices (9.1–10.18).

It may be that what Hebrews says is a rather bookish argument for Gentile Christians, contrasting the work of Christ with that of alternative helpers mentioned in Scripture and taking no account of the actual philosophical or pagan alternatives that Gentile Christians might consider. But the fact must be faced that there is nothing vital here that would answer and keep in the Church a Gentile Christian who, tempted and discouraged by hardship to give up his faith under the threat of renewed persecution, was considering Gentile alternatives of thought and worship. The argument would be much more relevant to a Jewish Christian wherever he lived. To him the Pentateuch would make a powerful appeal and the synagogue would be a serious rival to the Church.

A group of Greek-speaking Jewish Christians in Rome or any other place could find the argument forceful. Such a group could be the one that needed to be told by the author of Hebrews that the Levitical worship was based on sacrifices that were ineffective and outmoded.

This argument could be forceful even if written after the fall of Jerusalem in AD 70. Just as the period of the Babylonian captivity in Old Testament times was one not only of vigorous loyalty to the Law of God but also of literary activity to give effective written form to that Law, so the period after the fall of Jerusalem was one of intensive study of the Law and vigorous development and codification of the rabbinical traditions. It could have been a time when the biblical exposition of Hebrews had real relevance for Jewish Christians who were feeling the pull of the revitalized worship heritage of their ancestors.

It is just conceivable—but hardly more—that 13.13 was the

oracle that was vouchsafed by way of revelation' to 'approved men' of the Jerusalem church, telling them to leave the city before siege by the Romans could prevent their flight.[34] When the Christians of Jerusalem withdrew from the city, they were withdrawing also from active participation in the life of their people, and could be said to 'go forth . . . outside the camp'.

The difficulty with this conjecture is that Hebrews was written in excellent Greek, and it is not clear that there was a Greek-speaking church in Jerusalem in AD 66 to receive such a writing as Hebrews. The Hellenistic wing of the Jerusalem church had been driven from the city in the early days of that church (Acts 8.1)[35]; Stephen and Philip and their like-minded comrades were not allowed to continue their ministry there (Acts 6.1–8.40). James the son of Zebedee was martyred (Acts 12.2). Peter was imprisoned and then had to leave the city (12.3–17). Barnabas found his work elsewhere (Acts 11.22 ff.). Paul was widely considered to be the arch-enemy of his people (Acts 9.26–30). James the brother of the Lord was the leader at Jerusalem after Peter's departure (Acts 12.17; 15.13–21; 21.18) and his leadership was rather conservative, though not narrow or reactionary.

It thus is not easy to picture a church in Jerusalem in the sixties of the first century which could have been addressed in Greek as Hebrews addresses its recipients. If Hebrews went to Jewish Christians or to a church with a considerable proportion of Jewish Christians, it was more likely addressed to a church in another city, possibly but not certainly Rome.

The main point is that 13.13 with its command to 'go forth . . . outside the camp' fits a Jewish Christian church better than a Gentile Christian group. This does not mean that it was an orthodox Jewish congregation steeped in the Pharisaic tradition, but that with whatever liberal, syncretistic, or proto-Gnostic features it may have possessed, it was essentially a Jewish Christian group that could feel the pull of its Jewish heritage when it grew weary of suffering for its Christian confession.[36]

---

[34] Eusebius, *Church History*, III.5.3.

[35] Acts 8.1 speaks as though *all* Christians left Jerusalem in the face of persecution. However, the narrative in Acts refers later to Christians who apparently remained there, or at the very least soon returned there. It appears that it was the 'Hellenists' (Acts 6.1) who were harassed and expelled after Stephen's death. The Jewish leaders sensed in their views a threat to Judaism.

[36] Cf. Edgar J. Goodspeed, *An Introduction to the New Testament* (Chicago:

8. 'HERE WE HAVE NO LASTING CITY'

In these words of 13.14 we sense the problem of the Church and
the world, the Christian and his life in the world, or as it may also
be stated, the Christian and the city. For there is no indication in
Hebrews that the author found the relation of the Christians to
the Empire to be a pressing problem. It would seem that the past
persecution he mentions in 10.32–34 was not an official imperial
persecution of the Christians, but was carried on by local officials
or popular leaders outside of the imperial administration. But the
author does sense a problem in relating the life of Christians to the
city and its overwhelmingly non-Christian population.

This tension inevitably beset a minority group in the ancient
world. For although there were withdrawal groups both in
Judaism (cf. Qumran) and among Gentiles, the pattern of life was
overwhelmingly urban. People as a rule lived in towns and cities
rather than in isolated homes on separate farms. The population
which surrounded any church of Christians, therefore, would
almost inevitably be a city population. How many Christians
there were when Hebrews was written we do not know, nor could
we tell even if we knew exactly when and where it was written.
But the Christians were certainly a relatively small minority group.
The evidence of the New Testament is that they were essentially a
city group. This means that they were necessarily in close proximity
to the pagan world.

In such a situation, the Church had to make up its mind whether
its main interest would be to conciliate and conform to the community and its religious and social practices, or insistently pre-
serve its distinctive life regardless of possible reactions against it
from pagan neighbours.

There is no evidence in Hebrews that its author demanded
instant and complete withdrawal from normal community life.
We already knew from Josephus and Philo and Pliny the Elder
that there were withdrawal groups, especially the Essenes, among
the Jews in Palestine and elsewhere. We now know also from the
Qumran findings that there was a vigorous withdrawal sect
probably Essene in character, near the north-west shore of the

University of Chicago Press, 1937), p. 253: 'Christianity was coming to be an
old story. Apathy was pervading the church.' But this is not the whole story.
These Christians had been persecuted and could be again.

Dead Sea in the days of Jesus and Paul.[37] When we consider that John the Baptist started a wilderness-centred baptismal movement, that Jesus responded to John's preaching in the wilderness and evidently, at least according to John 1.35–43; 3.22–24, worked here for a time before John was imprisoned, that Jesus carried on a ministry that often, to say the least, had the roads and open country and lonely places of Galilee for its setting, we would not have been surprised if the author of Hebrews had urged people to leave the city, take to the wilderness or the country places, and reduce to a minimum their ties with city groups. Indeed, when we were studying the exhortation of 13.13 to 'go forth to him [Jesus] outside the camp', we noted that this could conceivably be an exhortation to follow the Qumran pattern of withdrawal. But that seemed to be the least likely of three possible interpretations of 3.13, and regardless of how we interpret 13.13, the fact remains that Hebrews thinks essentially in terms of a city setting both for the Church of that time and for the perfect social order of the future, 'the city which is to come' (13.14). That was the way of life that God had in mind for the final perfect setting of his journeying people.

The New Testament varies in its designation of this perfect city. As belonging to or, perhaps better, constituting God's perfect final order, though not yet given to God's people as the setting of their life, it is called by Paul 'the Jerusalem above' (Gal. 4.26). The Book of Revelation speaks of 'the new Jerusalem which comes down from my God out of heaven' and 'the holy city, new Jerusalem, coming down out of heaven from God' (Rev. 3.12; 1.2, 10).

So it is not surprising to find in Hebrews a reference to the promise of such a city. Abraham 'looked forward to the city which has foundations, whose builder and maker is God' (11.10); from the beginning of the life of God's people they have had this hope and promise. In a statement that practically equates the concept of

[37] On the Essenes and the Qumran community, see the summary in my book, *A New Testament History* (Philadelphia: Westminster Press, and London: SCM Press, 1964), pp. 52–57. Scholars are testing theories as to the possible relation of Hebrews and the recipients to the Qumran sect. See the bibliographical summary by Grässer, *op. cit.*, who notes, for example, that Yigael Yadin holds that the Christians addressed were former Qumran members who had not given up Qumran practices, and that Hans Kosmala thinks these recipients were Essenes or Essene-related Jews who had never come over to the definitely Christian confession.

a 'country' or 'fatherland' with that of a 'city', the author declares
that God's faithful people throughout their history have desired
'a better country, that is, a heavenly one. . . . God . . . has prepared for them a city' (11.16).

This promise has begun to be realized for the Christians: 'you
have come to Mount Zion and to the city of the living God, the
heavenly Jerusalem' (12.22). Fulfilment has begun for the
Christians, but it is by no means complete, and so 'we seek the
city which is to come' (13.14), the 'heavenly Jerusalem', the perfect
home for God's people of which the earthly city was never more
than a symbol or type.

In the meantime the Christians must maintain a detachment
from the city in which they now live. It makes no difference
whether their city is the earthly Jerusalem or imperial Rome or any
other earthly city in which the Christians now dwell, it is not the
city, the perfect home for God's people; that perfect home will
only be found in 'the city which is to come'. Therefore the author
of Hebrews insists that Christians keep a clear sense of the defects
and limitations of the city in which they now live. Essential to
their Christian stance is the attitude of confident hope, hope for
the city whose coming they eagerly expect.

So strongly does the author feel the need of not over-valuing
the city they now inhabit that his writing shows no note of
evangelistic zeal. He urgently presses his friends to hold fast to
their faith, but he never urges them to proclaim it to the world
all around them in the city they know in this age.

This is not a proof of a callous spirit, even though it does not
seem to us the best way to keep Christians vividly aware of what
they have and are promised in Christ. This is a group of Christians
who have known persecution (10.32–34). They have had the
courage to endure suffering, to keep their faith under public abuse
and ill treatment, to identify themselves with prisoners (who
probably included other Christians imprisoned for their faith), and
to accept the plundering of their property. All this they have
accepted in hope of a better future.

They are now urged to 'hold fast' to their confession (4.14;
10.23), either in the face of continuing ill-will from the public
around them, or in spite of the prospect of the renewal of persecution. They have had reason enough to know the sinfulness,
cruelty, and active hostility of the dominantly pagan city. But the

have shown a courageous solidarity under the test of persecution, and the author wants them to keep that loyal solidarity.

He wants them to show solidarity, for one thing, in regular assembling for common worship. The tendency of 'some' to absent themselves from that common worship and fellowship troubles the author (10.25); he knows that they need to keep the bond of Christian brotherhood strong especially in times when hostility from without actively besets them. They need the inner resources which can come only through common worship and mutual encouragement. They must not surrender to the pressures of the city; they must keep clear the awareness of that city's transience and imperfections and take heart from the promise of 'the city which is to come'.

Closely linked with this exhortation is the author's eschatological outlook. He does not undertake to picture in any detail what is to come, and like other New Testament writers he does not claim to be able to say just when the eschatological climax and conclusion of this world's history will occur. But the eschatological note is clear in his exhortations as well as in his theological discussion.

It is true that the author frequently contrasts the earthly scene and the heavenly scene, and some scholars have considered that his thought is essentially free from time consciousness and deals basically with the timeless contrast between this world and the heavenly world.[38] The awareness of a heavenly world is indeed clearly present in Hebrews. In part, however, what is said to be heavenly is something that God has prepared for men. 'He has prepared for them a city' (11.16), and it is to be given to them at the end of this age. In other words, the time factor is built into the very picture of the heavenly order, and it is radically wrong to try to interpret Hebrews in terms of a timeless eternity. The author of Hebrews certainly had a strong time sense in his understanding of how God has worked and will work. The heavenly Jerusalem is prepared for God's people and will be manifested in God's good time; it is 'the city which is to come'.

The author of Hebrews does not care to speak in detail of 'the

---

[38] See note 9. There is a good discussion of 'The Eschatology of the Epistle to the Hebrews' by C. K. Barrett in *The Background of the New Testament and Its Eschatology*, edited by W. D. Davies and D. Daube (Cambridge: University Press, 1966), pp. 363–93.

resurrection of the dead, and eternal judgment' (6.2), or of other eschatological topics. But throughout his 'word of exhortation' he sprinkles clear indications that he has a definitely eschatological framework for his thinking.

It was 'in these last days' that God 'has spoken to us by a Son' (1.2); like Jesus and the writers of the Gospels, he has an eschatology which has already begun to be inaugurated and is soon to be consummated. He speaks of 'the world to come' (2.5). Jesus 'has appeared once for all at the end of the age to put away sin by the sacrifice of himself', and he 'will appear a second time, not to deal with sin but to save those who are eagerly waiting for him' (9.26, 28).

This 'second time' will not be long in coming, the author indicates. The Christians addressed should worship together and encourage one another 'all the more as you see the Day drawing near' (10.25); the author sees the signs of the imminent coming of the final day of judgment which will bring the renewal of all things. As if to emphasize by repetition the nearness of the end, he quotes in 10.37 from the Greek translation of the Old Testament prophetic utterance Hab. 2.3, which he applies to his present situation: 'For yet a little while, and the coming one shall come and shall not tarry' (Hab. 2.3; the author of course understands 'the coming one' to refer to Christ).

13.14 fits into this expectation. This verse is not an explicit statement of eschatological hope such as we find in 10.25, 37. But it is in essential harmony with that statement. It says that we are not really at home in this sinful and transient world. We are no integral part of it. 'We seek the city which is to come.' The verb 'seek' means to search or seek earnestly for something; here in 13.14 it indicates a continuous, earnest, eager quest and desire for the coming of that perfect city which will be the everlasting home of God's people. There they will live in full fellowship with him and with Jesus his Son, the great high priest, who has made it possible for them to participate in this faith and enjoy its present and future gifts and blessings.

9. 'REMEMBER YOUR LEADERS . . . PRAY FOR US'

Only in chapter 13 do we read anything concerning the leaders of the Christians addressed (13.7, 17, 24). This gives no reason to suspect that this chapter is from a writer other than the author of chapters 1–12. It is only when he comes to give general exhortations and personal information that he has any clear reason to speak of the leaders. Up to this point he speaks in terms which apply to the group as a whole, and he often includes himself in the statements and exhortations he is led to express.

This earlier speaking to the Christian group as a whole is in full agreement with the way he refers to the leaders in chapter 13. In this last chapter, as in the earlier ones, he speaks to the entire group. Even here he does not speak to the leaders directly. He does not tell them to instruct the others concerning their duties in Christian living. In chapter 13, as in the exhortation passages of chapters 1–12, he continues to speak directly to the entire group of Christians he is addressing. He communicates with the leaders through the group; the group is to give his greetings to the leaders (13.24).

The exact relation of the author to the group to which he writes is difficult if not impossible to determine. He obviously knows these Christians personally; he does not write, as Paul does in Romans 1.9–15 and Colossians 1.3–9; 2.1, to persons he has never seen. On the contrary, he speaks of wanting them to pray for him, and he says that he has a more earnest desire for these prayers since he has confidence that through them he 'may be restored to you the sooner' (13.18–19). He has been with them before; he wants to return to see them very soon; he is so urgent in his desire that if Timothy, who has been released (from prison, it appears), does not reach the place where the author is in the near future, he will wait no longer; without Timothy he will return to see his friends and enforce by exhortations delivered in person what he here has written (13.23).

This need not mean that the author was a member of the local group he addresses. He does not imply that apart from his present journey, which for reasons he does not explain keeps him from immediate return to them, he is a permanent resident member of their church. A man of such obvious intellectual and literary ability would not be merely a member of the local group; he would be a leader. But in each of the three mentions of the leaders, he speaks of them as a group to which he does not belong. There is no hint that he is aware of being merely one of their local leaders.

His leadership evidently extended over a larger area than that of the group here addressed, though it seems quite evident that his area of interest and work included this group. He travels in the exercise of his leadership, and is at the time of writing occupied with some unexplained responsibility at some other place. It is highly unlikely that he himself is now in prison, as Timothy has been (13.23). But the situation where he is staying keeps him from an immediate return to the Christians he addresses, whose steadfast loyalty he is so deeply concerned to promote.

This is all that he tells us concerning himself. But he refers three times to the 'leaders' of these Christians to whom he sends this exhortation (13.7, 17, 24). The Greek word ἡγούμενοι is in form a present middle participle of the verb ἡγέομαι, which means to lead, to guide, or to think, to consider. The participle, used here in the masculine plural, thus means leading men. It is not a technical title but a description of the role these men played in the life of this group.

There is no indication that the leaders are divided into two or more ranks of varying authority. The term groups all the leaders together, with no suggestion of a division into separate classes, each with a different degree of authority and dignity.

The Greek word[39] was used 'of men in any leading position' and speaks of them as leaders or rulers; among its uses in that ancient time was its use to refer to leaders of pagan religious bodies. Among New Testament uses Luke 22.26 says that the leader must be 'one who serves'; in Acts 15.22 'Judas called Barsabbas and Silas' are described as 'leading men among the brethren'.

The word is used of Christian leaders in *I Clement* 1.3 (compare the synonymous compound form in 21.6), and this compound form is used in the *Shepherd of Hermas*, *Visions* II.2.6 and III.9.7. The word seems to refer to a more formal office in *I Clement* and the *Shepherd of Hermas*, but there is no indication of such a formal reference in Hebrews. The word designates leaders, but it does not indicate a formal office with a specific name, nor does it indicate in any detail the qualification or responsibilities or special dignity of those who hold leadership.

In particular, there is no hint that these 'leaders' were regarded by the author or the Christians addressed as priests in the Church. The strong interest of Hebrews in the Levitical priests and sacri-

---

[39] So Arndt and Gingrich, *op. cit.*, p. 344.

ficial ritual, in Christ as the great high priest, and in the high priestly offering in the heavenly sanctuary has almost continuously led Christians to think, perhaps unconsciously, that the author of Hebrews meant the leaders of the Church to follow in the foot-steps of Christ by acting in a priestly role. To think in this way, however, is to misunderstand completely what Hebrews has said.

In the first place, the author emphatically denies any saving efficacy to the Levitical sacrifices, even to the high priest's sacrifice on the Day of Atonement. Such sacrifices of animals and the offering of their blood could never take away sins (10.4).

The sacrifice of himself by Christ the true high priest was indeed effective, and it must always be gratefully so regarded by Christians. But the author hammers home with all the emphasis he can muster the crucial fact that this offering is a 'once for all' sacrifice. It can never be repeated; it need never be repeated. The one real priest-hood of which the author knows is this priesthood of Christ the great high priest, who offers 'once for all' the sacrifice for sins which is completely adequate and effective and can never be repeated. So the old Levitical priesthood is superseded, and there is absolutely no place in the Church for a new priesthood to be set up with a continuous chain of mortal human priests.

Christ is still the high priest; the benefit of his sacrifice is con-tinuously available to believers; he is continuously exercising his second priestly function, for he 'always lives to make intercession for' those he saves (7.25); so Hebrews knows nothing of any other priests in the Church; the only sacrifices Christians can offer are, as will be seen in our next section, Christian actions that are only figuratively called sacrifices and are to be carried out by all Christians. For the author of Hebrews the Church has 'leaders' but it does not have priests; it has only the one great high priest.[40]

This does not mean that the author of Hebrews speaks with any disrespect of the leaders he mentions. Quite the contrary. He speaks of them with genuine respect. There is no hint that they have ever been negligent in their duty or that they have been 'led away by diverse and strange teachings' (13.9). The author expects

---

[40] Nairne, *op. cit.*, pp. 154-9, recognizes that the author does not develop a theory of priesthood for the ministry of the Church, but finds such an appli-cation to the ministry and to other Christian relationships a logical and necessary step.

the Christians he addresses to show to these leaders the same
loyalty and respect that he expresses.

When we examine the three references to the leaders (13.7, 17,
24), it at once becomes clear that two separate groups are mentioned. Verse 7 speaks of former leaders, while vv. 17 and 24
speak of the present leaders of the group.

The former leaders whom the group are charged to remember
seem to be regarded as the founding fathers of the local group.
They 'spoke to you the word of God' (13.7). It surely can be taken
for granted that all worthy leaders past or present give sound
Christian teaching. So the author feels no need to defend the
correctness of what those earlier leaders taught. He seems rather
to imply that they gave the message in some special situation, and
it is likely that he has in mind their initial evangelistic preaching
in the community addressed.

It could be argued that the author is asserting only that the
former leaders carried on a faithful preaching of the true gospel
and that he is not saying or implying anything as to who founded
this particular local church or group of churches. But it seems
more likely that he refers to a special preaching by the earlier
leaders, and this would be their initial evangelistic preaching to
the Christians the author addresses.

These pioneer leaders are now dead. It might be argued that the
Greek word ἔκβασις, 'issue' or 'outcome', refers only to the good
results that one can still see in the worthy life of those early and
still living leaders.[41] But that is not the natural way to interpret
13.7. It seems that the leaders are now dead, and the manner of
their death is an example to consider and follow. It may be that
they were martyrs, who had showed their faith and faithfulness,
their loyalty to the gospel they preached, by the courage and steadfastness with which they faced death and died for their faith. But
the meaning more likely is that their worthy and loyal life continued in an exemplary manner to the very moment of their
(natural) death, and so their steady life-long faithfulness is now a
continuing challenge to their converts to 'imitate their faith'.

One strong reason for hesitating to conclude that they were
martyrs is that in 12.4 the author says to the church or local group

[41] Arndt and Gingrich, *op. cit.*, p. 237, say that the meaning of the phrase
here can be 'the end of one's life', but 'can also prob. be understood as (suc-
cessful) outcome, result of one's way of life'.

of churches addressed that 'you have not yet resisted to the point of shedding your blood'. If the leaders had been martyred, the author could hardly have spoken thus of the past history of this group. Therefore this reference would seem to be to the inspiring, exemplary, and long continued faithfulness of the early leaders of the group.

A chronological item may be noted in passing: 13.7 gives the definite impression that many years have passed since this group was founded by the sturdy leaders who first preached the gospel to them and then stayed on to give faithful pastoral leadership.

The present leaders likewise are proving worthy. They are regarded as men whose quality of leadership merits a response of obedience from the Christians under their care (13.17). They have a special responsibility and will have to answer to God for the way they fulfil it; they are 'men who will have to give account'. But the author seems fully convinced that 'they are keeping watch over your souls' in a worthy and helpful way. They should be appreciated and obeyed and shown the deference which their leadership plainly deserves.

The author wants these leaders to have the joy of a loyal response from the Christians they serve. It may be that the church members' general tone of weariness and their tendency to be lax in their loyalty, danger signals indicated earlier in Hebrews (12.12–13), are responsible here for the use of the double imperative: 'Obey your leaders and submit to them.' The double command may of course be simply an emphatic way of making a point, but it may be a light hint that the lax and weary spirit of this group calls for a firm reminder that they need to follow gladly and faithfully the instructions and exhortation of their leaders, who, it is implied, are doing their work well and deserve full loyalty from the Christians they are so faithfully serving.

The concise instructions in 13.24 to 'greet all your leaders and all the saints' is notable for two reasons. One has already been mentioned. The leaders are to receive the author's greetings not by a direct letter from the author but through the group. One could have expected the author to follow the reverse procedure, in which he would send his greetings to the entire group through the leaders. The way the author expresses himself suggests that he writes in a situation entirely free from any hierarchical atmosphere. It also suggests that he wants all the recipients to feel that he is writing directly to them; he wants them to recognize and respond to his leadership as they give their leaders his greetings. This act will also tend to keep them in close touch with those leaders.

The other notable thing in this final reference to the leaders is the twofold use of the word 'all'. The author assumes that not all of the leaders and all of the saints (that is, church members; all church members are consecrated, dedicated 'saints')[42] will be present to hear this message read aloud the first time. This need not suggest a divisive and sectarian situation among the recipients of Hebrews. It is much more likely that the use of the word all reflects the 'house church' situation that was far more normal in the earliest years of the Church than we usually realize (e.g. Rom. 16.5, 14–15; I Cor. 16.19; Col. 4.15; Philemon 2).[43] There were no church buildings at first. Christians had to meet as a rule in the homes of those believers whose houses were large enough to hold a group of worshippers and permit them to share a common meal.

A house church, a group of Christians meeting together regularly, might have a leader particularly active in that group of 'saints'. As the divisive situation in Corinth shows (I Cor. 1.12) this necessary separation of a growing local church into groups for at least part of their common worship and meals could have very bad effects. Cliques could develop and hostility or petty rivalry between groups could arise. The groups needed to keep in touch with one another.

It was therefore of vital importance that the greetings of the author be conveyed to 'all your leaders and all the saints'. He does not indicate the ways by which these groups might most effectively keep in touch with one another. But he has this problem on his heart, and so he intends to use the situation in which his message will be read to further the needed interchange of fellowship, information, and greetings among 'all' the leaders and 'all' the other Christians to whom he is sending his 'word of exhortation' (13.22).[44]

---

[42] The word ἅγιοι, 'saints', is used frequently in the Pauline letters, Hebrews, and Revelation. It describes Christians as 'consecrated to God' and so obligated to do his will. See Arndt and Gingrich, *op. cit.*, pp. 9–10.

[43] See my article, 'The Significance of the Early House Churches', *Journal of Biblical Literature* 58 (1939), pp. 105–12.

[44] 13.24 includes greetings sent by 'those who come from Italy'. This is another way of keeping the horizons of the recipients broad and their spirit 'ecumenical'.

10. 'TO DO GOOD AND TO SHARE'

Early in our study we noted the fourfold structure of chapter 13 with which the author, after concluding the discussion of his central theme, brought his 'word of exhortation' to a close. We noted that this fourfold structure was found in other New Testament 'letters'. It permitted the writer, in sending a particular message from a distance to be read in a Christian assembly, to touch on other aspects of Christian truth and life in which he wanted the addressees to prove loyal and diligent. It allowed for a formal benediction to give an impressive ending to his message, and then gave room for an informal group of greetings and personal messages, followed by a shorter benediction to provide the final words of the total writing.

The larger part of chapter 13 is given up to the wider range of exhortation which opens the fourfold structure. Our study may properly conclude with a brief study of these exhortations and instructions.

It is neither necessary nor right to find reflected in each exhortation a serious failure in the life of the recipients. It would be wrong to think that every imperative or exhortation puts the finger on a new and urgent crisis in their lives and fellowship. But each point is one which the author thinks the recipients need to take seriously if they are to live loyally and faithfully.

Because the imperatives cover a rather wide range, it is not necessary or possible to see a close logical link between each individual exhortation and the ones that precede and follow. Sometimes an urgent charge develops out of the preceding one, but this is not always the case. The common feature of them all is that they are important items to heed in order to maintain a worthy and steadfast Christian life such as the author wants these Christians to live.

The exhortations we find in chapter 13 deal with personal Christian life, relations within the Church, and individual contacts with the world outside the Church. The author is not concerned with a programme for radical renewal and transformation of the political and social order by a programme of governmental reform. He was a member of a small minority movement in a basically pagan society under a totalitarian pagan government in a world which he held to be in its 'last days' (1.2). So he had no proposals to offer for general social reform. To the extent, however, that what he had to say built integrity of life and concern for the welfare of others, he had a message that had lasting importance not only for personal life and face-to-face relations but also for social situations.

The main foci of his exhortations are as follows:

(i) 'Let brotherly love continue' (13.1). These Christians had shown such love under trying circumstances. They had been publicly abused and afflicted. Evidently some of their number had been imprisoned, and the others had shown their solidarity with the prisoners and had suffered confiscation of their property without wavering in their brotherly concern for one another (10.32–34). This had been real brotherly love, and that kind of love should 'continue', even if such harsh treatment again strikes the Christian group. It is possible that some of the prisoners mentioned were not Christians, but it seems likely that at least some of them were.

(ii) 'Hospitality to strangers' must not be neglected (13.2). The 'strangers' may include needy persons without connection with the Church, but to a great extent it has in mind travelling Christians previously unknown to the local Christians. Some of the latter travellers could be Christian leaders and messengers; others might be Christians travelling on business. The inns of that day were notoriously likely to be centres of pagan and immoral practices,[45] and so the provision of hospitality was more than an economic help and a convenient courtesy; it was a Christian service. Referring to the angels in such visits as those of Genesis 18.1–8; 19.1–3, the author reminds his friends that in showing hospitality one may receive a great blessing from the guest.

(iii) The charge to 'remember those who are in prison' (13.3) seems to refer to non-Christian prisoners more clearly than did 10.32–34. The Christian is to feel and express in action his solidarity with all who suffer and are ill-treated. He must not have the Gnostic lack of concern for what happens to some other men[46]; he is concerned with all who share the ills and trials of life in the body.

(iv) 'Let marriage be held in honour among all' (13.4). The

[45] Cecil John Cadoux, *The Early Church and the World* (Edinburgh: T. and T. Clark, 1925), p. 137, note 3, speaks of 'the foul moral atmosphere of the public Roman inns'.

[46] In the Gnostic view, which developed in full clear form later than the New Testament period, some men do not have the innate spiritual quality possessed by the true Gnostic.

word 'all' probably refers to all Christians, although in principle the author undoubtedly would like all mankind to support and practice purity in marriage. He is concerned here not only for the recognition that marriage is honourable, a position which excludes asceticism, but also for the maintenance of purity on the part of all who share the marriage relation. He condemns and threatens with judgment all 'immoral' persons, but since most persons were married he was especially concerned that adultery find no place in the Church.[47]

(v) He urges his Christian friends to 'keep your life free from love of money, and be content with what you have' (13.5). Love of money can be an ugly expression of deep-rooted selfishness.[48] It can keep Christians from helping their fellow-men who are in need. It can make them think of protecting their possessions rather than maintaining their solidarity with those who are outcast, despised, and ill-treated. (Compare 10.32–34.)

(vi) 'Do not be led away by diverse and strange teachings' (13.9). As we have seen, this refers particularly to special rules about 'foods' which, though we do not know the specific regulations in mind, were wrongly supposed by some to be of great spiritual help. The author emphatically insists that such practices are not spiritually helpful; indeed, they can be very harmful, for they can give men the deadly idea that it is their own practices, and not the free 'grace' of God, which is the real source of spiritual benefits.

(vii) In general the Christians are to maintain a wholesome degree of detachment from this world. It is not the perfect and permanent setting of life with God. 'Here we have no lasting city' (13.14). The old ties which believers had before they became Christians are not to govern the Christians' outlook and way of life. It is not that matter is evil or that this world is entirely bad: it is God's creation through his Son (1.2), and when not idolized it can be used in a helpful way to support and strengthen good Christian living. But the Christian has a great hope; 'we seek the city which is to come', which God will give and which will be our eternal home.

---

[47] On 'The Sexes and the Family' in the Apostolic Age see C. J. Cadoux, *op. cit.*, pp. 127–31, 191–4.

[48] See Matt. 6.24; Luke 16.13; and Paul's reference to covetousness as idolatry (Col. 3.5).

Since this is true, Christians must not become slaves to this present world, as though it were the best and final setting for the life of God's people. They must follow Christ rather than the old patterns, even if it means abuse (13.13).

(viii) The Christians addressed are not only to remember their former leaders who were worthy and faithful, but are also to obey and submit cheerfully to the guidance of their present Christian leaders, who are likewise devoted and faithful. There is no hierarchy in the Church as the author of Hebrews conceives it, but neither is there any thought of spiritual individualism-run-rampant and undisciplined anarchy. The Church consists of all its members, but they all are to respect and follow the guidance of its loyal leaders.

(ix) Offer the only sacrifices Christians can make. We have noted that in the new covenant there are no animal sacrifices and no mortal human priesthood such as we find in the Old Testament. Those ancient priests and sacrifices pointed to Christ as the one true priest, the great high priest, and to his offering of himself as the once-for-all and fully adequate and effective sacrifice. There is henceforth no place for any priesthood except that of Jesus or any blood sacrifice except Jesus' once and now past offering of his own blood in the heavenly sanctuary.

The leaders of the Church are not called priests. They offer no literal sacrifices, and the Church does not eat of the sacrifice for sins that Jesus offered when he offered himself (cf. 13.10–12). So in exhortation to the Church the author of Hebrews cannot urge them to present sacrifices such as were offered under the old covenant.

But by spiritualizing the concept of sacrifice the author is able to speak of two kinds of sacrifices which Christians can offer:

(*a*) 'Let us continually offer up a sacrifice of praise to God.' This is a sacrifice made by 'lips that acknowledge his name' (13.15). This was not a new idea previously unexpressed in Hebrews or the Old Testament. It is the 'acceptable worship' which we are to offer to God (12.28). It is the fulfilment of what Psalm 50.14, 23 urged: 'Offer to God a sacrifice of thanksgiving. . . . He who brings thanksgiving as his sacrifice honours me' (i.e. God).

(*b*) 'Do not neglect to do good and to share what you have' (13.16). Vocal praise to God is an essential in the Church's worship, but it is no substitute for tangible expressions of wholesome, helpful, brotherly living; God desires 'steadfast love (AV: mercy) and not sacrifice' (Hos. 6.6). In the great formal benediction of Hebrews (13.20–21) the prayer of the author is that the Christians he addresses may do God's will. That was what Christ did: 'Sacrifices and offerings thou hast not desired. . . . I have come to do thy will, O God' (10.5–9). 'To do good and to share' is the indispensable manner of the Christian life, and 'such sacrifices are pleasing to God' (13.16); they are what he wants men to do in obedience to him.

All of these pointed exhortations in chapter 13 show the author's pastoral concern and his spiritual understanding. They are not alien to the aim and exhortations of the earlier chapters. Their wide range of concerns overlaps to some extent those of chapters 1–12. What is said ties in with the Levitical framework of the earlier discussion, but it rises above that framework. It shows how the old system of animal sacrifices finds a worthy spiritual and moral replacement in sacrifices of praise, obedience, and active, helpful brotherly love, a love concerned to minister actively to all who know suffering and need.

4

CONCLUSION

THE key to understanding the writing which we commonly call 'The Letter to the Hebrews' is given with the discovery of the fourfold structure of chapter 13. After concluding the specific discussion found in chapters 1–12, the author turns to a series of imperatives and exhortations concerning a number of subjects which he thinks should receive the alert and continual attention of the Christians he addresses. This rather wide range of instructions is followed by the formal and rather lengthy benediction found in 13.20–21. It might seem the proper way to end the entire writing, but the author has still some personal news items and messages to include, and only after he has spoken of them does he finally conclude the writing with a shorter benediction.

Other New Testament 'letters', especially several of the Pauline collection, show a similar pattern in their closing portion. Possibly Paul set this pattern. Possibly it arose without conscious literary planning as the inevitable result of preparing a message to be read aloud to a congregation (or congregations) located at a distance from the city where the writer finds himself.

However the pattern originated, it already existed and was available for the author of Hebrews. He uses it to give varied exhortations which he would give in person and possibly in a more informal way if he were with the Christians addressed, but must now in his time of separation from them include in his larger work to make sure that the recipients do not neglect them. The formal benediction shows the author's awareness that he is sending a message to be read aloud at a meeting for worship to the Christians who are the special object of his concern. The added greetings and information and the final benediction constitute a more informal addition to the preceding formal discussion and exhortations. The four parts form a definite literary pattern.

Once this pattern is discerned, there is no longer any reason to suspect that chapter 13 or a portion of it was a later addition to the preceding section. The writing has a fundamental unity, as is seen when the themes of chapter 13 are studied carefully and the agreements in thought between chapter 13 and chapters 1–12 are noted. It cannot be expected that every exhortation of chapter 13 will be fully paralleled in chapters 1–12, for it is a basic feature of the four-fold structure at the close of such a writing that the added exhortations cover a wider range than the scope of the main discussion. But a basic agreement in the thinking and concern of the parts of Hebrews could reasonably be required, and such agreement has been found and noted.

This understanding of chapter 13 gives us a better picture of the writer, his purpose, and his pastoral concern. The imperatives and appeals in chapter 13 join with the extensive hortatory sections of chapters 1–12 to show that this work is indeed a 'word of exhortation' (13.22).

We find in Hebrews a Christian leader who uses skilfully the Levitical regulations, the ceremonial aspect of the Mosaic Law, to set forth by the use of typology the unique and superior gospel of salvation by the self-offering of Jesus Christ. But though he shows great interest in skilful biblical exposition, it soon becomes clear that his real concern is the faith, the spiritual vitality, and the steadfast faithfulness of the Christians addressed. He wants them to withstand the temptation to laxity and fading loyalty; he wants them to realize that what they have in Christ is supremely important and so is worth every effort and sacrifice.

This Christian leader and author presents a unique Christology. Jesus is the divine Son of God. Above all, he is the great high priest who met temptation, was perfected through suffering, and through his offering of himself once for all won complete salvation and so provides the gifts to meet every believer's need. The author takes the human life and struggle of Jesus seriously, but in general agreement with the entire Apostolic Church he finds the climax and key to the Christian message in the Lordship, authority, and intercession of the risen, exalted, and glorified Christ. But all this is not merely an advanced theological lesson. It is a message set forth to nerve the Christians addressed to stand fast and receive the benefits of this unique work of Christ.

The gospel story as reflected in Hebrews contains a definite eschatology. The author has a strong time sense, and he senses that he is living 'in these last days' and that in 'a little while' the end of this age will come (1.2; 10.37). This too is stated not because of a merely technical theological interest but to give his Christian friends the vivid sense that eternal and ultimate issues are at stake in their decision whether to hold fast and be faithful in the face of the indifference some comrades may show and the ill-treatment they themselves may suffer.

The priestly imagery is likewise used to serve an urgent and practical purpose. Jesus Christ fulfils the promise in the Old Testament sacrificial system; he is the one true and effective priest; he is the one once-for-all and fully effective sacrifice; there is no place for any further sacrifice for sins and so no place for a continuing priesthood. The Old Testament priesthood finds its fulfilment in Christ, and so the Church is led to a non-priestly worship in which sacrifices for sins are not continually offered by a succession of priests. The idea of sacrifice as it applies to the Christians is spiritualized to mean sacrifices of praise, doing good, and sharing what one has with those who are needy and suffering.

The author has a vivid sense that this world is not perfect and is not the lasting home of God's people. He has and urges a life pattern that avoids complete involvement in this world and this age. But he does not urge an ascetic or monastic withdrawal from the common life of men. He rather shows a deep concern that Christians be alive to the existing need and suffering, that they feel their oneness with needy and suffering folk, and that they continue active in relieving such need and suffering in every way they can.

The author of Hebrews is a question mark in many ways.[1] Many questions which we continually ask about him and his situation we cannot answer with any confidence. Who was he? When did he write? Where? To whom? In just what situation in his own life and in the life of the Christians to whom he was writing? Such questions still puzzle us and he remains a rather elusive figure. Essentially he is to us what he has written. And that is a great deal to know and to have. It can spur modern Christians to renewed and increased awareness of what their faith can mean to them and what their faithfulness can mean to others.

---

[1] Albrecht Oepke, in *Das Neue Gottesvolk* (Gütersloh: C. Bertelsmann Verlag, 1950), pp. 17–24, notes the 'unsolved questions' concerning Hebrews, and seeks 'the way to the solution' not in 'the journeying people of God', as Käsemann does, but in 'the new people of God'.

INDEX OF NAMES

INDEX OF BIBLICAL REFERENCES

OLD TESTAMENT

NEW TESTAMENT